WARDROBE

To Dad and Grandpa for their inspiration during my
formative years, and to my husband, Victor, for all his love,
encouragement and involvement.

To all ladybirds!

WARDROBE

DEVELOP YOUR STYLE AND CONFIDENCE

Susie Faux

with Philippa Davies

PIATKUS

© 1988 Susie Faux with Philippa Davies

First published in 1988 by
Judy Piatkus (Publishers) Limited,
5 Windmill Street, London W1P 1HF

British Library Cataloguing in Publication Data
Faux, Susie
  Wardrobe: the working woman's guide to
  1. Women's clothing. Fashion
  I. Title   II. Davies, Philippa
  746.9'2

  ISBN 0–86188–726–3

Designed by Dave Allen
Fashion illustrations by Lynne Robinson
Line drawings by Paul Saunders
Photography by Sven Arnstein
Cartoons by Min Cooper

Typeset in 10/12pt Linotron Century ITC Light by
Phoenix Photosetting, Chatham, Kent
Printed and bound in Great Britain at
The Bath Press, Bath, Avon

CONTENTS

INTRODUCTION

I love to see a woman look good and to know that I've played a key part in helping her achieve that look. It is a very rewarding feeling, and one which I am lucky enough to experience almost every day. I have two shops in London's West End where I show women how to choose clothes which, as well as making them look more attractive, help them project an image of individuality, style and confidence. And if a woman looks confident, she will feel more confident in herself. The one follows the other. Early on in my career a magazine article referred to me as a 'sartorial psychologist'. The description is apt, and all my colleagues at Wardrobe share my enthusiasm and responsibility in this area.

I have been in the fashion business all my life. I was born into it. According to my mother, I started caring about my appearance before I was a year old; apparently I refused to wear the dress she'd chosen for my first birthday party! My father and grandfather were top quality ladies' tailors, and they soon had me sewing hems for pocket money. In return, they taught me about perfection and detail, and it was in their workrooms that I developed my eye for style and quality, cut and colour. I also learnt what women wanted from their clothes and saw what they could achieve through their appearance.

I started Wardrobe 15 years ago to meet a need. I realised that as well as wanting to buy clothes women wanted to improve their total appearance and to present themselves as 'credible' and caring. This need seems greater now than ever and I have written *Wardrobe* for everyone who would like to share in my experience. It will help those of you who, like myself, wanted to return to work after years of looking after children but had lost confidence and felt out of touch. It will serve as a revealing reference and guide for those of you who are starting out on your career and want to be as competitive as you possibly can. It will also act as a quiet reminder for those of you who are at home most of the time and know just how easy it is to let yourselves go. And for the older generation, who may have the time to experiment with clothes and make-up but who are ignored by most of the shops, magazines and designers, it should be a welcome source of information and advice.

My philosophy is a driving force behind this book. I believe that most women need, and are able with a little help, to make much more of themselves and how they look. It is not too difficult to discover why they often fail to look their best. To dress well, with only a small wardrobe of versatile garments, entails a number of skills, and learning these skills is what this book is all about.

In my shops and at my seminars we emphasize the importance of training your eye to identify what really suits you, and we aim to do the same in these chapters, through words, drawings and photographs.

First you have to recognize and appreciate your own individuality, so that you can learn how to select clothes which express this, and yet marry well with your lifestyle and workplace. In a word, your image must be 'appropriate' – your clothes must compliment you, feel comfortable and be able, if necessary, to take you from office and meetings to theatre or party or home.

Next we show you how you can develop an eye for cut, cloth and colour, for what suits you, your shape and colouring. Yes, it can be learnt! We show you how to build up a capsule wardrobe that really works for you, how to accessorize it and how to put together your total look. Finally, we show you how to put all these principles into practice when shopping – which most definitely is an acquired skill. (Here I speak as a one-time impulse buyer!)

A major benefit of the guidelines I give in this book (guidelines only, because there can be no hard and fast rules) is that *you will save time and money*. You'll make fewer mistakes, and by choosing clothes that are exactly right for you, you will end up needing fewer garments, which are themselves more versatile. Less really can be more. By knowing exactly what you want and need, you will be far more economical with your time, and your shopping will be efficient and rewarding.

I hope that by absorbing the information in this book you will be in a far better position to assess your relative assets and imperfections and to develop the image that you want to present. The right image will bring with it a sense of style and a supreme sense of confidence. You will have a smaller wardrobe than the one you own now, but it will be of good quality and it will work for you at all times. It will, I am sure, help you to gain the confidence and credibility you need in order to maintain your competitive edge. I truly believe that a confident appearance can only enhance your career and, more generally, your lifestyle. In our shops we always feel elated and excited when we see and hear of our customers' personal and professional progress mirroring the improvements in their appearance. It so often happens. 'Remember,' as a friend of mine is fond of saying, 'you deserve everything you get.'

CHAPTER ONE

First Impressions

BUT
ITS A
STATEMENT
NOT A
GARMENT.

It is surprising how many women today fail to place any great emphasis on the importance of clothes. The British and Americans lag far behind Italy and France in the sartorial stakes. To the more cosmopolitan Europeans, a British woman looks frumpy and eccentric, displaying a lack of attention to clothes, hair and make-up. American women, on the other hand, tend to *over*dress, or stick to a work 'uniform' which denies individuality. This is a shame, for first impressions – whether business or personal – are so vital and influential.

I believe that the years of the Sixties were largely responsible for this, and that that decade had a catastrophic effect, in some ways, on the development of fashion style and 'appearance awareness'. The pill and the women's movement helped increase equality for women, and interest in clothes was deemed frivolous. Intelligence was demonstrated by a rejection of a smart appearance. If you were serious about 'life's true meanings', then you certainly did not have time to think about your grooming.

This preoccupation with higher things fizzled out in the Seventies, but its detrimental effect on style has been longer lasting. Many women who grew up during the Sixties still feel that a preoccupation with clothes is a sign of superficiality, and this attitude has transmitted itself to ensuing generations. Any readers harbouring reservations like this would be well advised to study Alison Lurie's *The Language of Clothes*, a fascinating insight into the psychology of clothing and image. It's interesting that academics are almost expected to look scruffy – the ill-groomed professor and the drab bluestocking. University students were also *expected* to look scruffy – perhaps partly because of the paucity of their grants, and partly because their minds were set on higher things! Nowadays, in a competitive job market, job-hunting undergraduates are realizing that their abilities can be only enhanced by presenting a good appearance.

We have to wear something, and it always amazes me when people try to declare 'I don't care about clothes' by looking unkempt and badly dressed. They must be hoping that when they walk into a room, other people will react to them as though they had their eyes closed! Their refusal to consider clothes as important will not prevent them being reacted to and assessed on their appearance by others. We are so strongly visually orientated that the choice we display by our appearance always makes a statement of one sort or another. In this book, I hope to give you guidelines on how to make this the very best sort of declaration.

APPEARANCE MATTERS

Appearance *does* count! You can use it to boost your confidence in yourself and in your abilities. It is undoubtedly your most powerful form of communication. This is particularly significant when there are cultural or even language barriers to overcome. If someone has an obviously different background to you, and is not speaking in their first language, then what you see is what you judge. Lacking other bases upon which to operate, both participants in the meeting are likely to be searching for signals in the other person's appearance that indicate there is going to be empathy between you.

Firstly, if you like yourself, you show it in the way you look. We all know that it's much easier to like someone if they obviously like themselves. Similarly, if someone sees themself as a long-suffering drudge, then they'll start to look like one. This is a self-perpetuating vicious circle: the lower their self-esteem, the worse they look, and the lower will be the regard they receive from others. Far too often, people who are depressed reveal their depression through a lack of care in the way they look. Their inner turmoil is expressed through what we see.

Advertisers have been aware for decades just how strong our response is to the visual image. Often we buy products for the first time simply because we liked the *look* of the person using the product in the television commercial or magazine photograph. These people (predominantly actors and models) are carefully selected so that a certain (preferably large) section of society will identify with them. They create a strong image – the considerate dad, the blooming young mum, the angelic child and so on. We make a whole set of value judgements, many of which are subconscious, when we look at people or things. We marry people, make them our friends, and employ them, frequently because we liked the look of them. There has been extensive academic research done on this.

'Not caring how you look is but a brief step away from not caring what you do or how you treat people. And surely, if you treat yourself with contempt, you're going to have little thought, care or compassion for anybody else?'

Lynda Lee Potter
writing in the *Daily Mail*

'In marketing, you need to identify what target you want, and what target your competitors are after. How you present yourself should reflect your ability to sense what people need and want to see – if you're not sensitive to this then you're unlikely to inspire confidence in clients...'

Jan Pester,
Marketing Director

Michael Argyle, a well-known sociologist and broadcaster, sums it up by suggesting, 'The body a person has, or perhaps *the body image he succeeds in presenting*, has a marked effect on his feelings about himself and on his behaviour towards others.'

At its most basic, your appearance shows how healthy you are, and to what extent well-being is a priority for you. Modern science can perform miracles on our naked selves – we can fake-tan our skin from bottles, get hair removed or coloured, have faces and breasts lifted, tummies tucked – but not all these procedures are cheap, painless or safe. However, there are limitations in the changes you can impose on your naked self. The basic skeletal framework cannot be altered, for instance, so wide shoulders or hips have to be accepted. But thankfully, you do have a complete choice over what is put on your body – your clothes.

Often, though, with the range of clothes available, what to put on your body can be a bewildering decision to take. Mistakes are made on a multitude of levels, and I often meet women who are articulate, intelligent and ambitious, yet they lack awareness and confidence about their appearance. 'Why do I always get asked to make the coffee when I go into the boardroom?' queried one young, highly qualified accountant. We looked in the mirror together and saw a woman in a drab cardigan and polo-neck sweater. Exchanging them for a smartly tailored suit, stylish earrings and subtle make-up was a revelation. And an American university recently carried out some interesting and relevant research, following the careers of two groups of women. One group dressed very ordinarily and made no special effort to look good, relying totally on their qualifications: the other group, with similar qualifications, made the effort to dress in a way that was suitable to their jobs, if not a little *more* than the job required. When the researchers went back five years later, the women who had taken a pride in their appearance, and had felt that this was an essential part of their career development, had all done better than those who had not bothered. So appearance does matter, and clothes do the professional woman make!

CLOTHES AT WORK

Getting a good job is not easy. Getting to the top, or running your own business, however small, is very tough. It takes perseverance and professionalism, and the constant drive to always be one step ahead of the competition. This means that you have got to *look* more successful than the other person, even if you are just starting and going out after your first job or contract. You could call this a confidence trick – but it works!

If you are on the way up the ladder, then a good appearance

will give you confidence at those all-important interviews. You will show that you have good taste through your choice of clothes. And if you are clean, well-groomed and attractive, with thought and attention given to detail, you will be regarded as a woman who will use these qualities in her work and dealings with people.

You must also feel comfortable in your clothes: it can undermine your confidence and distract you if you're worried about how you look or feel. If you are in a meeting in a skirt that is too tight and too short, you will feel uncomfortable both physically and psychologically. Your mind needs to be utterly on the business in hand, secure that the way you look is effective and appropriate. If your appearance reflects consideration for yourself, then you will give the impression of being able to consider others. Similarly, if you are in a business dealing with people – the service industries or personnel etc, careers in which women do particularly well – it is as important to look professional and composed at your 5 o'clock meeting as it was for the first appointment of the day.

Always dress for a job that is a position *higher* than the one you are already in, if you are starting off on a new career. A personnel director at one of our seminars confided in me that she had been extremely sceptical of our service at the outset. After she had seen us reappraise the women – clothes, make-up and hair – she said that she would have offered them twice the salary she'd thought of pre transformation! Therefore you can increase your 'value', quite literally, by looking good.

A word here about 'power dressing', a term often derided by the press. I like to think of it as 'responsibility dressing'. There is no doubt that if you want to be successful in a career, then this involves taking responsibility and the judicious use, rather than abuse, of power. It need not involve being aggressive, intimidating or ruthless. Power and femininity are not incompatible; indeed the ability to bear children is an astonishing power. So ignore those who sneer at you for responsibility dressing – they almost certainly carry a sneaking suspicion that had they presented themselves in a better way they would be further up the ladder by now!

Similarly, customers sometimes tell me that they couldn't polish up their appearance because their boss would resent it. In my experience, the more enlightened female boss is likely to ask you where you got your new look – and go there herself! If she is disparaging, then she is probably insecure about her own appearance and ability, and not likely to promote you anyway. As my husband, a management consultant and business school professor, says, 'First-rate managers hire first-rate people; second-rate managers hire third-rate people.' So remember, if you look like a first-rate individual, you are far more likely to be hired by that first-rate manager. When a position needs filling,

'Employers are quite willing to pay more for people who already look the part. There is the inference that employees who care about themselves will care about their jobs.'
Susan Bixler,
The Professional Image

'I think it is important at the start of a career to regard grooming and style as an intrinsic part of your armoury of skills and to invest a relevant part of your salary to keep your image polished, just as you would believe it necessary to pay for a course in, say, computing or French.'
Audrey Slaughter,
Your Brilliant Career

your appearance can give his or her imagination a subtle prod in your direction!

Assuming you are already on your way up the career ladder, the reasons for presenting yourself well are slightly different. The better you look the more you will be thrust into prominence, whether it is meeting the public, new clients or the media. You are more likely to be asked to make presentations (however much the prospect might terrify you). If you are confident in your appearance, this gives you an opportunity to impress clients and colleagues, as well as prospective employers or employees. If you are the interviewer, you are a highly paid visual representative of your company so it is important to present an attractive image to encourage the very best candidates to want to work for you.

According to sociologists in the study of what has been called 'impression management', the first three minutes of a meeting are the most important. Thus the emphasis on 'first impressions'. In a business meeting, the appearance of both individuals is a key factor in deciding behaviour and how much formality is used. Appearance defines the situation and lays the ground rules for the interchange. Alison Lurie comments: 'To wear the costume considered "proper" for a situation acts as a sign of involvement in it, and the person whose clothes do not conform to these standards is likely to be more or less subtly excluded from participation.' Just as a business associate might feel uneasy about having a meeting on a park bench, rather than in the accepted environment of an office or boardroom, if someone wore jeans or glitzy clothes to a meeting, she would convey the impression that she lacked judgement and understanding of the situation, and that there was a wide gap between her own values and those of the other person.

Your appearance can help you earn admiration from your employees and subordinates. By dressing in a smart stylish way, you can set a good example for them to follow. If your clothes are good quality, than they can act as a tangible incentive for those below you to achieve more, earn more money and dress in the same quality clothing!

For a woman who has started her own business, or is in business with her husband, looking good is just as important. In any sort of business, you are selling something, and your appearance must make people want to buy. When closing a deal, appearance is particularly important. The fact that you look confident and successful could create that extra impetus that makes your customer 'buy'. Even if money is tight at the outset, try to present as prosperous an appearance as possible. Customers will assess the quality and efficiency of your business by what you present, and people like to be associated with success. I frequently hear women say, 'I'll buy the suit when I

'As a prospective employer, if someone came for a job in dirty or untidy clothes, I would think, "Oh you're sloppy", and I would have a bad impression. If they had a double first I would pursue it and ask them why they came to an interview like that – is it some kind of protest against work? I would try to get that sorted out. If someone comes clean and tidily dressed, to me it shows respect for the job and the people they work for.'
Detta O'Cathain
quoted in *Flying High*

get the contract.' But getting the contract can be that much easier if you've bought the suit beforehand...

Very few women are successful in politics, and I suspect part of the answer might lie in their uneasiness and uncertainty about how to depict themselves in a high-media-profile lifestyle. An aspiring politician once told me that she could not present herself as a smart professional – which she *was* – because this would widen the gulf between her and her electorate in a depressed inner-city area. I suggested that a voter who wants to put trust and hope in a politician is far more likely to do so for someone who looks successful and prosperous than someone who looks exactly like they do. We frequently seek 'role models' whom we can admire and aspire to, and the voter will think 'If she can do that for herself, then she can surely do something for me!' This explains why female politicians who look professional are considerably more successful than those who look like dowdy housewives. For a professional appearance does not in the least imply a lack of sympathy: which doctor would you rather see, the one in jeans with straggly hair, or the neatly-coiffed one in a suit? I know which one I would choose...

A fine appearance will never compensate for a lack of abilities, and dressing smartly will not transform you into a managing director or government minister overnight. Clothes can camouflage your naked self, enhance your individuality, and bring out your positive qualities, but they do not disguise your true self. They can, however, help you on the journey to the top. The signs are promising for the promotion of women into middle and senior management in the future, and more companies are consciously choosing to offer women key positions. For women to go into the twenty-first century showing that they are of comparable stature to men, they need to make a different, but equivalent, professional impact.

> 'We have to look better than men in business, because there are always some men who want to dismiss women and their influence at work. If we look like the little woman at home, we give them the opportunity to do this...'
>
> Marjory Glen,
> Abbey Life

TODAY'S WOMAN

The number of women in management positions today is rising quickly, although they still make up only a small percentage of the management workforce. More than ever, women are being given the *opportunity* to prove themselves professionally. However, we often have problems about just how we should present ourselves. Should we imitate the behaviour of men and try to be aggressive, with little show of emotions? Should we dress for business in severe pin-striped suits with heavy briefcases – in an 'imitation man uniform'? I believe that many women are prevented from reaching the top because they send out such a confusion of signals about how they see themselves, through their clothes. The accountant who was always asked to make the coffee in the boardroom, for instance, was dressed in cosy, homely clothes which would have looked more appropriate in the kitchen or lounge. To be quite blunt, the most suitable setting for her would have been curled up by the fire, knitting!

You need to dress in a way which makes you look completely comfortable with the role that you are playing, and which reassures others – men in particular – that you are confident and competent in this role. Decades ago, a woman's appearance merely reflected the class that she belonged to, whether she had a rich husband, and what he and she considered was their social standing. Now, however, barriers between social classes have broken down, and women do not now depend on their men to dictate their spending power or status.

More and more women are going back to work after having had children, or they are putting off motherhood until they are in their late thirties, with successful careers established. As it is usually the woman who takes a break in her career for the responsibility of parenthood, this puts a certain pressure on her to achieve more in a shorter time. To do this, and to overcome areas of resistance that still exist to women's promotion, a woman needs to look as, or more, professional than her male counterparts.

And when you do make it to the top, you become highly visible. You can hardly pick up a newspaper today, without reading an article about successful businesswomen. Magazines and companies frequently run competitions for women who are high achievers. It is very important to look good if you are to be exposed to media attention, and this covers 'appearance' on all levels. We are living in an age when communication through video, car telephones, fax and telex is tremendously important. The way we communicate through dress, voice and body language is also under far closer scrutiny. Many jobs that are advertised demand 'excellent communication skills', and many companies run training courses to refine these qualities in their employees. However, when you walk into a room full of strangers, *the most immediate and direct instrument of communication that you have is still your appearance.*

In 1992, European trade barriers are due to decrease even further, and doing business in Europe will become more commonplace. In the face of language and cultural differences, your appearance becomes a most potent sales instrument. At the time of writing, new video telephones are being developed. When these come into widespread use, even people at home will have to maintain a good appearance! Yes of course you could turn off the video transmitter, but wouldn't Monsieur le Blanc or Signore Blanco wonder what you were trying to hide?

'Image-consciousness' in itself is becoming increasingly important. Politicians in Britain and elsewhere are now being packaged in a way that is much closer to their American

'I adore the Englishman's scruffiness. The more interesting the man, the less interested he is in dressing well – as if it's stylish not to be stylish – puritanical, as if it is practically immoral to spend money on themselves. The scruffiness looks fine here in Britain but it can be embarrassing when abroad.'
Carla Powell,
wife of Charles Powell,
Private Secretary to Mrs Thatcher

counterparts than has been the case previously. Every aspect of their image and that of others in public life, can be put under scrutiny from hairstyle and colour to the way they use eye contact. Designers, stylists and communications trainers find themselves giving eagerly sought advice to clients ranging from politicians to royalty and pop stars. For some of the less talented performers, 'image' is all, and they rely heavily upon it for success. The international media attention given to a princess who has decided to concern herself with fashion has been incredible. Her 'image' is a constant source of fascination.

Today, and following in the wake of our European counterparts, we have begun to appreciate the value of design for its own sake, rather than something that was done to 'make things work'. We view items from clothes to toasters as much for their aesthetic appeal as their functional one. 'Lifestyle' shops, selling everything from cutlery to lingerie exude a certain image, aimed at a certain market. Designer accessory shops flourish. People are opting to buy a few designer or quality clothes – that carry status – rather than buying large wardrobes from chain stores.

'Yes, but how does all this affect me?' you might ask. Well, to my mind, these changes are full of promise for a stylish future. Heightened awareness of the power of the visual image and design should mean that the woman who takes her appearance seriously has so very much more going for her.

CHAPTER TWO

CLOTHES TALK

Why wear clothes? Most basically and practically, because we need to keep ourselves warm and protect our bodies from the elements. As a result, we tend to choose them according to the climate that we live in. The social mores – the morality or religious values – of our society also play a large part, dictating that particular parts of the body are covered. Political and economic values will also affect what we choose to wear, and these will reflect in how the wearer is viewed by others. All these are enshrined in the three Cs of clothes – Cut, Cloth and Colour – which, I believe, are the most vital elements of the best clothes and the most effective dressing. Clothes do indeed 'talk', revealing volumes about the individual wearing them.

The elements above are, in turn, closely associated with the time or era in which one lives. It's often difficult to be objective about an age in which you live, but hindsight shows clearly how clothes reflect social mores. This century has seen considerable change in the role of women in society and their political, sexual and economic independence, and these changes have been reflected in clothing. Let's have a look at some of the most significant and enduring influences on our clothes in the twentieth century.

BACKCHAT

Broadly speaking, when times are hard, clothes are likely to be worn for their practicality and low cost, therefore they tend to be fairly functional and simple, without excessive use of cloth or detail. In more affluent times we can afford to own more clothes of better quality, so some of them can be frivolous or impractical, serving as affirmations of our prosperity.

At the beginning of this century women were clad in elaborate restricting clothes, symbols of their family's wealth and status; and fashion, as we understand it today, was largely the preserve of the wealthy. The First World War had no immediate effect on clothing styles, though women came to know far greater employment than ever before, especially as nurses. Many women continued to work after the war – the 'secretary' had arrived – and skirts began to get shorter, and more practical for travelling. The suit had already become popular as sportswear – for golf, for instance – and it gained in favour as an outfit to wear to work. 'Land girls' had worn trousers during the war, the first time women in any number had sported these garments, and after the war the practicality of clothes became a far greater consideration.

In 1918 women over 30 got the vote, and ten years later the vote was given to women over 21. The Twenties show more clearly the effects of the aftermath of war on clothing styles. Coco Chanel revolutionized the concept of high fashion, designing clothes that were simple and functional, yet strikingly elegant. Her neat suits and frequent use of jersey were widely copied, causing her to declare, 'If there is no copying, how are you going to have fashion?' She was responsible for making the suit an indispensable and practical choice of clothing for smart women. The growth rate in literacy and printing technology meant that her designs were popularized through women's magazines, an ever-increasing source of influence on clothing throughout the first half of this century.

The Twenties and Thirties heralded the golden age of cinema, and film stars in their glamorous outfits were widely copied. The Thirties line was softer and more elegant; the strapless evening dress become popular as the sun-bathing vogue took off. And when Schiaparelli showed shoulder pads in *Vogue* in 1933, they were to stay fashionable from then on. I'm often asked whether shoulder pads are going to go out of fashion, to which I reply, 'As they've been popular for over 50 years, I think that it is extremely unlikely.' Indeed, as far as tailored clothes are concerned, it is very difficult to get a good 'line' without pads or shaping in this area. Have you ever seen a man's suit without padding or shaping in the shoulders?

During the Second World War, with the focus of life shifting to the necessary and the expedient, changes in fashion slowed down. Clothing factories became increasingly efficient because they were mass-producing uniforms. Women's war-time utility clothing was serious and practical – plain fitted jackets with square shoulders and short skirts. There was little excessive use of cloth or detailed features, and nothing that would impede your progress to the nearest air-raid shelter. Again, for practicality – and warmth probably – slacks were worn by women who drove ambulances and trucks, and they have stayed popular ever since.

'No man can possibly realize how women are influenced by the clothes they wear. Put even the plainest woman into a beautiful dress and unconsciously she will try to live up to it.'

Lady Duff Gordon,
Ladies Home Journal, 1944

In 1947 Christian Dior launched his 'New Look'. He described it as a reaction to a 'poverty-stricken, parsimonious era'. The New Look had softly rounded, padded shoulders, was fitted over the bust and at the waist, with long full or gored skirts. The excessive use of material was condemned by Sir Stafford Cripps, the president of the Board of Trade. It was a feminine, elegant look after the deprivation of war, and undoubtedly much needed.

The effects of war continued through the early Fifties, and society expressed its need for security and order in the way that women dressed. Cut became more generous. Circular coats and dolman sleeves were worn with narrow or full skirts.

Many women who had worked during the war continued to do so. And going out every day, it was important for them to look presentable. They had their own money to spend. The period between the Second World War and the late Fifties was characterized by clothes that were smart and structured, implying a grown-up, responsible attitude towards life. The middle classes grew, and it was very important to be 'correctly' dressed (hence the rise to prominence of the cocktail or 'little black' dress). While researching this chapter, I chatted to an elderly gentlemen on the theme of fashionable dress in London. He said sadly: 'I knew London had changed when I walked into Claridges and there was a lady *without* a hat on'!

In the late Fifties clothes became more extreme; exaggerated full skirts with petticoats, beehive hairdos and stiletto heels, or drainpipe jeans and pony-tails. In 1957 Givenchy introduced a version of the shift dress, a shape that became dominant in the Fifties and has stayed fashionable ever since.

Significantly, the early Sixties saw a major shift of emphasis in fashion: from catering for the woman in her twenties through to her forties, to an over-riding concern and focus on the young. The world had discovered the teenager.

The new youthful confidence was expressed by mini-skirts, trouser suits and see-through blouses. The futuristic designs of Quant, Pierre Cardin and Courrèges made women look aggressive and asexual. Unisex dressing had arrived. Many of the major British designers and couturiers lost credibility at this time; their clothes seemed very classic and dull in comparison. The Italians took over the market with their *prêt à porter* collections, consisting of a new elegance with a little more interest, and British fashion went into a decline from which it is only now recovering.

At the same time men and women started to look to the East for philosophical inspiration and clothes stopped being signals of wealth and status. People expressed their reaction against materialistic Western values by dressing in kaftans, Afghan coats and sandals. Flower-power dresses and heavy embroidery on shirts and trousers showed a spirit of rebelliousness

OPPOSITE PAGE
LEFT
The classic Chanel suit.
TOP RIGHT
The New Look.
BOTTOM RIGHT
The Mini skirt.

towards the dark suiting worn by the 'conventional'. Concern for the environment and its inhabitants, and a stress on spiritual values, were reflected in dress. Real fur became unpopular, and in the early Seventies slaughter of certain endangered species, like vicuna, actually became illegal.

The early Seventies heralded a confusion of styles as women came to terms with their new freedom. An economic recession hit, and the punk movement, with shorn heads, earrings, tattoos, torn clothes and safety-pins, expressed the discontent and rebellious spirit of the young.

The last two decades have seen strong fashion trends emerge and disappear, and the atmosphere now is really one of 'anything goes'. However hard fashion editors and manufacturers try to enforce a certain hemline length, more and more women choose to buy what suits them and what is appropriate for what they do. That's not to say that I think we should ignore the influence of fashion; we should *adapt* it to our own individual requirements.

Cut, Cloth and Colour

To adapt fashion in such a way, you need to be able to work out what your own requirements are. I analyse this in a practical sense in Chapter Five when I tell you how to evaluate your present wardrobe, but the psychological aspects of clothes – what they say about their wearer, both to herself and to those meeting her, and what she wants her clothes to say – are more relevant here.

As well as giving vital first impressions in our visually oriented society, clothes and appearance can also reveal even deeper insights into people. They tell others about your lifestyle, confidence, wealth – even where you live. City dwellers, for instance, tend to wear sombre tones and angular shapes, reflecting the grey buildings of their environment, whilst country folk favour greens and browns, blending in with their landscape. Simplistic maybe, but true.

CITY DWELLERS TEND TO WEAR SOMBRE TONES AND ANGULAR SHAPES.

How, then, can clothes be read? Every garment has three determining features – the way in which it is *cut*, the *cloth* in which it is made, and its *colour* – and each of these, individually and/or together, can be very revealing. To me, cut, cloth and colour are the three most crucial criteria when deciding on the purchase of any garment – or, in my case, collection. As a fashion professional, my eye is obviously very finely tuned, and I can judge on *one or two garments only* whether a designer collection (which might include 150 garments) will be suitable for me. The cut, cloth and colour of those items are as revealing as can be a sample of handwriting. You may not think this is relevant to you, but we all, whether we know it or not, and however unsophisticated we may be in terms in fashion, make judgements, using those general cut, cloth and colour guidelines.

Cut will determine how much fabric is used in making a garment, how many pieces of different fabric are used, how close or loose fitting it is, and how much detail is added. In the cut of clothes we will see soft or straight lines, structure or lack of it, so an image softened or toughened accordingly. In general, a more 'formal' cut – a tailored cut – is the one for business, and this in turn, to a certain extent, dictates the cloth used. The unstructured cut of casual clothes makes them less appropriate wear for more formal activities such as business meetings, interviews and presentations. The working day is usually structured in terms of tasks which need to be performed; most companies are tightly structured in terms of managerial hierarchy; this order is reflected in the working woman's choice of tailored clothes with a clearly structured cut, for her everyday work wear.

The cloth in which it is made will affect the weight and texture of the garment, therefore how warm it is and how smooth or creased it looks. Stiff cloth will not move as easily as a looser weave, and the fibres in the cloth will determine how the body reacts to it. Cloth also creates impressions: silk looks sensual, expensive, even slightly exotic; tweed, in contrast, suggests rural, homespun values. The cloth of a garment can show how much money someone is prepared to spend on their appearance, and how much they wish to communicate their success to others. Ostentatious displays of wealth are usually associated with excessive furs, large amounts of jewellery, and obvious designer labels. But more subtly, garments in cashmere and silk (which most of us know are expensive) can suggest sufficient funds to buy cloth that feels beautiful to wear.

When there is a shortage of a certain cloth, its market value increases, and if someone is wearing a lot of it, they are obviously wealthy. A garment which is generously cut with ample cloth will cost more than a skimpy item, where the manufacturers have economized on cloth to keep costs down. I think this is the reason that clothes can often look 'cheap' – the original concept of the design used better quality cloth in far more generous proportions. However, on fitted clothes, the expense comes from the amount of seaming and skill used by the experienced designer and pattern cutter.

Cut and texture of cloth also determines how much of our bodies we expose. Obviously, a low-cut chiffon blouse will send out very different signals from a high-necked paisley pattern one, and will create a very different impression. In casual clothes, which tend to convey an impression of comfort and relaxation, the cut is unstructured, and large pieces of fabric are assembled together with little detail. The cloth used is

THE UNSTRUCTURED CUT OF CASUAL CLOTHES MAKES THEM INAPPROPRIATE FOR BUSINESS MEETINGS.

comfortable to wear, and easy to wash and keep clean. The best sort of casual clothes come in colours that are easy to accessorize, that do not need careful matching. Hence the popularity of denim for casual wear.

The colour of clothes reads very strongly and can reflect how one is feeling: large blocks of bright colour, or bold garish patterns will attract attention; subtler shades make the wearer seem less prominent. We also associate certain colours with certain qualities – gold and purple with power and exclusivity as well as wealth; red with danger; pink and peach with frivolity and femininity, immaturity even. Blue tends to suggest coolness and lack of commitment; yellow a strong urge to appear sunny-natured; and the earth colours – greens and browns – suggest calmness and solidity (not necessarily desirable if you're intent on the top in a more creative profession). These are inevitably broad generalizations, as there is a huge range of shades and tones under the umbrella title of a colour name. There is an increasing interest in colour, however, and studies are being made of its significance and the psychology behind it.

Some colours have 'rich' connotations. A smooth fabric like silk and white or cream is obviously going to require a lot more cleaning than a brown needlecord. The implication is that you are wealthy enough to have your clothes cleaned frequently, or alternatively that you have a lot of time on your hands for maintaining delicate fabrics.

Cut, cloth and colour all indicate whether you are 'operator' or 'ornament'. Lots of detail on clothes, impractical colours and cloth will tend to indicate that professional considerations do not come uppermost. Frothy frills and flounces are just not practical work wear for most of us anyway, just as extremely high heels and very tight skirts are obviously not designed for movement. The wearer would seem to see herself as relatively static – her prime function ornamental or decorative – rather than as someone who is effective and on the move.

Some people want to attract attention, to make themselves stand out from the crowd. They want to convey the impression that they don't really care one iota about what others think of them, that they're saying, 'I'm an individual and I'm going to create an overpowering impression of this through the way I dress.' These people will probably opt for loud dramatic clothes, cut in an extreme way, in strong colours. Often large women do this, primarily because they can rarely find interestingly suitable clothes for business in their size. At its most extreme, these extroverts can choose to look as though they do not see themselves fitting in with society, but often this statement creates its own sort of uniform. Just think of teddy boys, punks and skinheads. 'Uniforms' depersonalize the individual and make the wearer's actions answerable to what the uniform represents, rather than their own choice. Sadly, sometimes we choose to make an overpowering statement through our clothes to compensate for what we feel are inadequacies in our personalities – like the introvert who wishes she could lose her shyness, and so dresses flamboyantly, and spends all evening withering with embarrassment.

Clothes also illustrate where you see your status in society. The 'old school tie' is the best example of an item depicting status and membership of a certain group. For 'upwardly mobiles' certain designer labels carry a lot of status. Nowadays, even high-street shops represent images of an idealized lifestyle and an appeal to certain sets of values. More than likely, you and your friends and colleagues with similar social economic values will buy at the same shops, be they designer boutiques or high-street chains. This too is a form of 'uniform' and sends its own messages out about self and style.

Even accessories say a great deal through their 'cut' or shape, 'cloth' or material in which they are made, and colour. They can suggest individuality and express personality – tiny pearls suggesting traditional values, interesting chunks of gold, creativity.

Choices of cut, cloth and colour should always be made appropriately for *you*, taking into consideration all the quirks that make you an individual. In later chapters we will examine how to make these choices, and what they signify.

'Even those people who insist that they despise attention to clothing, and dress as casually as possible, are making quite specific comments on their social roles and their attitudes towards the culture in which they live.'

Desmond Morris,
Manwatching

CHAPTER THREE

WHERE WE GO WRONG

Many women avoid making the way they look a priority for themselves. It's all too easy to impose strong limitations on the way you see yourself, and the way you think others see you. In this chapter I want to look at some of the prejudices and conditioning that exist against and within women as well as some of the excuses used by those women – which may well include you – as to why they dress less effectively than they might. Stereotype dressing must be considered as well. Once all of these are identified, you can then abandon them, and proceed to positive action – to improving the way you look, and making your appearance mean business.

PREJUDICES AND CONDITIONING

Women working in a managerial capacity are a relatively new phenomenon for many men. If they have been brought up to believe that 'a woman's place is in the home' then they can find this breed of woman frightening. I once overheard a man at a business school remarking on a group of women about to embark on a course there. 'Do you see those intimidating women?' he asked a colleague, a slight note of alarm in his voice. The group of women to which he was referring was the most unassuming, impoverished looking and ill-groomed imaginable! He was seeing them in the knowledge that they were women *in business*, and had a strong preconceived prejudice against them. If your appearance sends out signals that reminds male colleagues of their maiden aunt or teenage daughter, then they will find it difficult to appreciate your function in the workplace. If your appearance oozes professionalism, on the other hand, they will easily accept you.

I think women are too sensitive about looking intimidating, and confuse looking aggressive with appearing competent and capable. Looking smart will signify that you know how to present yourself, that you are competent in your grooming, and this will, in turn, influence others as to your competence in other areas. A male lawyer once said to me, 'A woman who looks good and is intelligent and articulate is dynamite in any organization.'

To overcome any remaining prejudice against you as a woman in the workforce, you need to look secure and comfortable in your role as a professional person, rather than sending out signals that you should be at home, doing the chores.

We have a strange attitude to success. 'Success' and 'ambition' have been words tainted with distaste, particularly when applied to women. We've been tempted to think that these qualities have to be associated with an aggressive, pushy behaviour style, and that qualifications should speak for themselves. Any attempt to *look* as though you want to be successful has been dismissed as 'brash'. Many women seem to think if they look too good or successful, they've got further to fall if they fail, and believe an unassuming appearance can act as a safety net, when no one will expect too well from them. But people are now beginning to realize that you can be ambitious, and can use your confident appearance as an aid to getting to the top.

Some women are uneasy about becoming and looking successful because of the effect it might have on their husband or boyfriend. Your personal life can be dramatically affected by success or failure in your professional life, and some men find it emasculating to be married to a woman more successful than them. A woman who does earn more than her husband is an exception – women on average salaries earn 25 per cent less than their male counterparts. Neither are the tax laws always conducive to the high-earning female executive's marital bliss!

Trying to play down that success by looking dowdy – the ploy used by far too many women – doesn't really work. Looking harassed and fraught (even if you are) will only reinforce the impression that you've a lot of responsibilities. If you think about it anyway, your husband's failure in a business venture would almost certainly put as great a strain on your relationship as your success! Fortunately, more and more men are happy that their wives have careers. So whilst he might be moaning about the microwave meals, he's probably very proud of you!

'I never used to dress to the level of success that I had achieved. I think many women are rather surprised when they succeed professionally; they don't expect to do so, and they fail to dress to the appropriate level because they are surprised to be there...'

Marjory Glen,
Abbey Life

Excuses

Over the years, many of my customers in the shop and at our seminars have given me reasons why they avoid improving the way they look. Here are some of the justifications that I've heard most frequently.

THIS, OR AN ELECTRIC RADISH-FLOWER-CUTTER?

'... BUT I COULDN'T SPEND THE MONEY'

Many women feel guilty about spending money on themselves. Often conditioning leads you to expect others to be dependent on you – husbands, children, parents even. You spend your money on what you consider necessities – food, clothes for the children, videos, cars, holidays abroad and school fees. You feel guilty about spending money on yourself; somehow it's far easier to justify buying a household gadget. If you buy something for yourself it's best if it's a bargain.

Do you delight in telling others the cost of a garment bought in a sale – but keep very quiet if you've spent rather a lot of money on it? I'm often guilty of this, and halve the price of something I've bought when telling my mum!

In contrast, Italian and French women feel guilty if they do *not* buy good clothes or have a regular manicure. Our attitude to life is obviously a lot more serious and puritanical, and it is also very short-sighted. By investing in your appearance, you are also investing in your professional future.

'... BUT I DON'T HAVE TIME'

Caring about your looks can easily be relegated to a low level of priority, especially if you have a job to do, a home to run and a husband and children to feed and clothe. You feel guilty about spending time 'titivating' when there seem to be so many other important things to do. Yet I've already established just how important your appearance is, and I will demonstrate how, by using 'scheme and analysis' (see Chapter Six), you can care for yourself using time economically.

Trying to add to a badly-managed wardrobe can be very time-consuming. It is often difficult to find an appropriate item to fit in with an overly large and haphazard collection of clothes. This book aims to show you how to save time by training your eye, using the criteria of cut, cloth and colour when you buy. In business you operate most effectively by taking time to consider action, rather than by charging in and behaving rashly, and your wardrobe can be run along similar lines – planning and projection if you like!

'... BUT WHAT ABOUT THE DEMANDS ON ME?'

Sometimes, if you feel that a particularly large number of demands are being made on you by family, friends and colleagues at work, visibly demonstrating a lack of concern for your appearance can act as a defence. If you dress in a jumble of shapes and colours, you are not likely to exude confidence and therefore are less likely to be asked to shoulder greater responsibility, though you are probably well fitted to deal with it.

The sad fact is that the longer you continue to look a mess, the more inadequate you will feel and become. Start to think and act constructively about the way you look, and you will find other people and yourself responding more positively.

In the way that an unkempt impression might lower your expectation of responsibility, creating a professional impression can raise it. But perhaps you have been avoiding making your appearance matter because you have a sneaking suspicion that your abilities cannot match up to it? Are you afraid that if you were given more responsibility you couldn't live up to expectations? If so, you need to investigate ways of building up your confidence and self-esteem.

'... BUT I DON'T WANT TO SEEM VAIN'
Most of us would hate to be thought of as vain and self-obsessed. Indeed, people who are constantly thinking and talking about their appearance are not generally regarded as interesting company. They can seem to have immature personalities, because their identity is completely defined by their looks, which act as a beacon of attraction. The contents of teenage magazines reflect the preoccupation of teenage girls with their looks: a fitting age in which to experience a search for identity and an awakening sexuality.

Self-obsession arises from insecurity, and is quite different from self-esteem which arises from confidence, and a balanced view of your achievements and shortcomings. This self-esteem shows when you care for your appearance.

'... AND I DO WANT TO BE TAKEN SERIOUSLY'
You might feel that what you do is far more important than how you look. The legacy of the Sixties contributes to this thinking as does the antiquated idea that brains and beauty are rarely found in the same woman. Does obvious attention to your appearance really reflect superficiality and detract from your abilities?

Perhaps you think that women, for far too long, have been assessed by the way they look, rather than how they think. Maybe you do not want to gain recognition in this way. I'd suggest that you could be confusing the importance of appearance with sexually provocative dressing (which I'll talk about later). This certainly will get you the wrong sort of attention!

'... BUT WHAT ABOUT MY FIGURE FAULTS'
We can easily choose to ignore how we look because an aspect of ourselves – large frame, big nose or bottom, unmanageable hair even – becomes a target on to which to project our insecurity. If you refuse to come to terms with your size, for instance, you may well wear clothes that are ill-fitting and can even make you feel physically uncomfortable, hampering your movement. You will look as though you literally 'don't have the measure of yourself'.

Sometimes if something about the way we look is making us

especially unhappy, a large bottom, for example, then the particular problem can take on a significance that is quite out of proportion. If you've failed to win an important contract, for instance, you might decide to go out and buy something new to wear to cheer yourself up. Whatever you try on will look unsuitable because whenever you look in the mirror, your large bottom prevents any garment looking good. Feeling negative about yourself, you use your particular 'problem' as an excuse to give up on the way you look. With greater awareness of proportion and expert advice, every woman should be able to minimize what she considers to be her bad points. There are some guidelines in Chapter Four.

You can also postpone tackling your appearance until you've dieted and are a dress size smaller. And when will this happen? I like to take a realistic approach, whereby we confront our defects and capitalize on our assets *immediately*. Just thinking more positively and looking better in clothes that fit your *current* size can help you to start losing weight.

'... BUT WHAT WILL PEOPLE SAY?'
If you start to take your appearance more seriously, people around you are likely to comment on it, and you'll have to deal with this. If you are single, your colleagues will, in all probability, start quizzing you about your social life, which could be irritating and not what you intended. Point out to them that you've decided to improve your appearance for yourself, rather than letting them assume there must be a new man in your life.

Of course we all do seek approval from others, to varying degrees. Changing your appearance will inevitably cause reaction amongst your peers, but secure, constructive friends will always support you. Always bear in mind that any detractors would probably like to make the very same improvements themselves.

'... BUT I DON'T KNOW WHAT TO WEAR'
The sheer quantity of clothes available can cause confusion, and make choosing what to wear seem a very complicated business. Because women usually have several roles to play – career woman, wife, mother – they need a range of clothes that encompasses all the activities these roles involve, be it playing with a messy three-year-old, cooking dinner for a husband's colleagues, or attending a meeting in the boardroom. As a result, women employ a clothing 'system' which sends out signals far more expressively than men's, and it is also far easier to make mistakes. With little time to spare, you can easily grab a garment originally bought as 'costume' for your 'role' as mother – a casual tracksuit top perhaps – which, worn in the wrong setting, at work, makes you send out confused signals. Does she want to be here developing her career, or

does she secretly long to be at home with the kids? You'll feel uneasy too. I'm sure you've experienced having dressed in a hurry, rushed to work, and then not 'feeling right' in an outfit all day.

On the other hand, the man's role and his working outfit – the suit – offer limited scope for variation. Men have far more of a 'uniform' look for business – the shapes of the tailored jacket and trousers have undergone only minor adjustments since Victorian times. Even in a casual working environment, men wear clothes based very much on the shapes of the suit. Often their only concession to fashion is their tie. The shapes of clothes that women have to choose from, however, are considerably more varied, with skirts, dresses, trousers and jackets and, within these categories, infinite variations. We as women have a much wider range of garments in our 'supply' – what is available for us – and a much larger number of roles for which we are 'in demand' – for what we are needed. This makes it more difficult for us to achieve 'compatibility' in choosing clothes. I'm sure most of us have been through the dilemma of whether trousers or a sleeveless summer dress are appropriate wear for a particular appointment.

Another reason for the dilemma is that there are far fewer women in public life than men, and thus we have few models to identify with and think 'That's the way to do it.' Women in top management are still, if you like 'pioneering', both in the way they operate and in the way they present themselves. They must be the 'role models' of the future.

'. . . BUT WHAT IF I STAND OUT?'

Working in a male-dominated environment, you may feel that caring for your appearance will make you more prominent as a *woman*, reinforcing the difference. This is anachronistic. The more you present yourself well, in accepted workwear, the less likelihood there is of your being regarded as an alien being. Your clothes are 'speaking' a universal language of professional competence.

Sometimes, if you are unsure about asserting yourself over others, you may decide to dress 'down' to their level, mistakenly believing that this will increase your acceptability. In fact, the most likely outcome is that they *lose* respect for you – it's much easier to take orders from a smart person than a scruff! *Breaking the Glass Ceiling*, a study of the barriers to women reaching top management positions (written for the Centre of Creative Leadership, Greensboro, North Carolina), studied 'derailed executives' – those who showed great promise that was never realized. The survey reported that women were more likely to be cited for having a poor image, and one-third of the female executives were said to have an image problem.

'The wish to merge into the background is pathetic, not because it is undignified but because it does not work. Since there is no mistaking a woman for a man, not even one in a tailored suit, why enter the straitjacket to start with?'
Leah Hertz,
The Business Amazons

'I think the fact that women are noticed in business more than men – because there are less of us around – should work to our advantage. It's an opportunity for us to stand out and make our mark, because we are in the minority. Women should feel positive about this.'
Jan Pester,
Marketing Director

STEREOTYPE DRESSING

You need expert advice to help you with legal or medical problems, and many women also need expert guidance on their appearance. Working women, who are using time and energy in their careers, have little scope left for sitting around, reappraising how they look. Very often, and especially after their late twenties, they tend to stick to the same look, what they *think* suits them. Here's a lighthearted look at some characteristic ways in which we can get it wrong.

THE MINI MAN TENDENCY

Pinstriped suits and ties, clumpy flat shoes, severe hair styles and heavy briefcases contribute towards this look. Friends and colleagues are likely to feel uneasy about your attitude towards your femininity – you will be sending out strong signals of insecurity. You don't need to look like an imitation man to succeed in business, and a softer style will make you and your colleagues feel far more comfortable.

THE FRIGHTFULLY FEMININE TENDENCY

Frills, bows, lace and silky dresses with Peter Pan collars make up this look. It's a doll-like overstatement of femininity that is as artificial as the 'mini man' look, and makes your appearance as intrusive. Besides which, that over-coiffed hairstyle takes an awful lot of work every morning! You might bring out the Sir Galahad in men, but they will always regard you as a woman first, *then* as a business equal. Simpler lines and shapes that are soft, yet less fussy and detailed, will be more effective.

THE DEPRESSINGLY DOWDY TENDENCY

The dowdy look oozes practicality and staidness. Well-scrubbed faces, sensible shoes, simple hair-cut with fringes, cardigans, narrow-shouldered jackets and A-line skirts are the main features. The trouble is that you are likely to be regarded as boringly dependable, and without flair or creative ability. By throwing your 'drab-rags' to the wind, and dressing in a sharper, more modern mode you could well find your career and personal prospects much improved.

THE INTERNATIONAL JET-SETTER TENDENCY

This look reads glamour through Farah Fawcett hair, an all-year-round suntan, lots of jewellery, obvious designer labels, strong perfume, over-generous make-up and long pointed nails. The signals sent out suggest that a great deal of time, money and attention have gone into the picture, and that the wearer of this look is determined to stay young. It also reveals that she lacks confidence, needing such obvious status symbols. To be successful in business, it is far better to look more quietly and subtly successful in high-quality cut and cloth.

> '*I have a hatred of being a feminine version of a man. You can wear perfectly ordinary, feminine clothes. Pinstripes and lapels do not make you any better at your job.*'
> Jennifer D'Abo,
> Businesswoman

THE CONSCIOUSLY CREATIVE TENDENCY

This look is usually sported by women who work in the media. Voluminous hairstyles (often shaggy perms), tight jeans tucked into boots, raunchy leather jackets and high fashion garments characterize this look. Black clothes are very popular. . . . The look is a very loud announcement that you are *creative*. But do you need to try that hard to show it?

THE SIXTIES SURVIVOR TENDENCY

Ethnic influences, in jewellery and material – heavy African beads and Madras cotton for instance – are the basis here. Skirts will be long and full and shoes flat and round-toed. This look usually goes with long straight hair and little make-up and, from the point of view of business dressing, it is dated and unsuitable. The arts and craftiness of a home-made brightly coloured sweater is perfect for walking the dog at weekends but looks unsuitable in a working environment.

These are gentle pointers as to the direction in which you might be getting your style wrong. Many of you will not show any of these tendencies, but I'm sure that you will recognize the traits in others. It's often as well to know what *not* to do as it is to know the best way of doing something . . .

'She looked as if she had been poured into her clothes and had forgotten to say "when".'
P.G. Wodehouse,
Novelist (1881-1975)

CHAPTER FOUR

TAKING A LOOK AT YOURSELF

'A stylish woman has good clothes that work for years.'

Ralph Lauren

Before re-planning your wardrobe, you need to step back and take thorough look at yourself: at your figure and size, at the proportions of your body, and figure faults – and good points, of course – and at your colouring. No rose-coloured spectacles, please. You need to be ruthlessly honest and know what's best for you, what doesn't suit you at all, and how you can emphasize or camouflage good or bad features.

SHAPE, SIZE AND PROPORTION

Clothing can do a great deal towards emphasizing your good points and playing down the bad ones. Most people look a lot better with their clothes on than off, even in these body-conscious days; thus it is vital to buy clothes for the shape and size that you are *now*, rather than the one you would like to be. If you are determined to diet or change your shape, then give yourself a time period in which to achieve this. If it proves impossible, then accept yourself, *like* yourself, and resolve to capitalize on what already exists. Remember that *you* are the norm, not that gazelle-limbed model in a magazine.

When a customer looks at herself in an outfit in a full-length mirror, I always know which part of her body she likes the least. It will be the part her eyes go to first, showing her concern that it is adequately camouflaged. So, before you read any further, take a good look at yourself from every angle. Where do *your* eyes go first? Tummy or bottom perhaps? If you have difficulty analysing your shape then ask a truthful friend, whose opinion you can trust. Make a mental note of your assets and defects. In the following sections, I am going to run through the body from the head downwards, with suggestions on how you can train your eye to emphasize or detract from various aspects, through your clothing choices.

However, it is most important to consider your body's proportions *as a whole*. Giving hard and fast rules for a figure feature in isolation is risky, as large hips could be balanced by a small waist and large shoulders, or vice versa. So look at your figure as an overall picture with comparison in mind. Your vital statistics should help.

Get a very clear mental picture of your shape. If your shoulders are sloping and narrow and you've wide hips, for instance, then you're approximately triangular. Putting an inverted triangle shape in terms of your clothes over your triangular body will obviously redress the balance. Similarly, if you've square shoulders, a thick waist and comparatively narrow hips then your silhouette will be squarish. If you choose clothes that are sheath-shaped – narrowing in the middle – then you will only emphasize your thick waist. Sometimes what seems like camouflage only adds emphasis, so try out different shapes of clothes and see what they do for you. When you go clothes shopping bear in mind your shape, and look categorically at the shape of garments. This will help train your eye as to exactly what suits you.

Cut, cloth and colour have a place here too, in terms of proportion. Large-framed women will look out of proportion in clothes with a lot of small detail, such as collars, pockets and trimmings. They will carry generously cut clothes well. Their smaller colleagues, on the other hand, can look drowned by large pieces of fabric hanging loosely. The detail of their clothes always needs to be proportionate to their size. A neat compact cut will work well on someone whose physique can be similarly described.

A coarse textured cloth on a woman who is very delicate and fine featured will keep its shape and stiffness on the body, and will look incongruous on her. It's rather like packaging a beautiful perfume bottle in an orange box, or a lace handkerchief in newspaper. On a larger woman, smooth sheer fabric will cling to curves, perhaps accentuating bulk in a way she would rather underplay. A bulky cloth like a thick velvet will always be assembled with thick seams, and will not make for a streamlined appearance.

Patterns, too, can reinforce the impression that your physique makes. A small person can look overwhelmed in a large bold print, and get 'lost' in it. A larger, more dramatic person will carry it with flair.

Light bright colours leap out to the eye, and, whether you are large or small, they will certainly get you noticed. These bright colours also make the area they cover seem larger – so be warned! More sombre, subtler shades may take a little longer to get noticed, but they will allow the person *inside* the clothes to be seen more clearly. Keep bright colours for blouses and scarves.

'If a woman walks in and people say what a wonderful dress, she's badly dressed. If they say there's a beautiful woman, you know she's well dressed.'

Elsa Schiaparelli,
Fashion designer
writing in the 1940's

PEAR SHAPED FIGURE
Needs building out at the shoulder line, so that the shoulders are no narrower than the hips.

TOP HEAVY FIGURE
Needs a slightly wider shoulder line than hip line. A lower neckline reduces the heavy effect caused by a solid block of fabric on the top half.

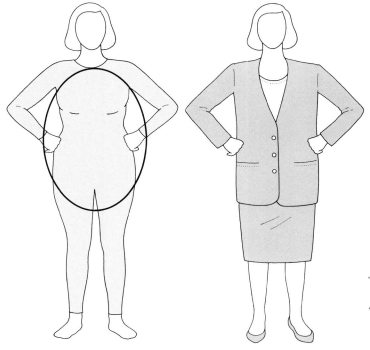

PLUMP FIGURE
Needs a straight rather than fitted garment, so that attention is not drawn to the waist. The jacket is long and straight, which brings the hip and shoulder line into balance. The neckline should not be too high.

STRAIGHT FIGURE
Needs soft clothes which drape flatteringly to emphasize curves. The waist should be accentuated if possible, by wearing a wide belt.

THE HEAD

If your head looks small compared to your body, then a closely cut hairstyle will emphasize the contrast and your frame will look larger. A haircut with more volume will look better. A petite frame will be accentuated by masses of hair, making the head seem bigger by comparison. We shall deal with hair and face shapes later on in Chapter Nine.

THE NECK

A short neck will be emphasized by long hair, the lines of the hair shape pulling the eye downwards. A roll collar or wide slit neckline will create a strong line across the body, where you least want to draw attention. Instead, give an illusion of length by keeping the neck as bare as possible and going for scooped necklines. Avoid cluttering the neck with short chunky necklaces and scarves. Much of this applies to thick necks too, as again you want to create an illusion of length. Draw attention to the ears by wearing chunky earrings, and create more apparent length in the neck by wearing V-shaped necklines.

A long neck is very graceful, but it can look disporportionate and 'ostrich-like'! In this case you want to avoid tight roll and polo necks which will only emphasize the narrowness. Generous cowl necks and wide soft folded collars will create horizontal lines that cut across the neck, shortening it. Revers and stand-up collars will work in the same way.

A scraggy neck is best dealt with by choosing a loosely tied soft neckline, a mandarin collar, or a roll-neck that stands slightly away from the neck.

TOP LEFT
Avoid wearing scarves or chunky necklaces around a short neck, as they will draw attention to it.

TOP RIGHT
A scooped neckline will help to give a short neck the illusion of length.

BOTTOM LEFT
A low neckline will emphasize a long neck and should be avoided.

BOTTOM RIGHT
Wide soft folded collars will create a horizontal line which helps to shorten a long neck.

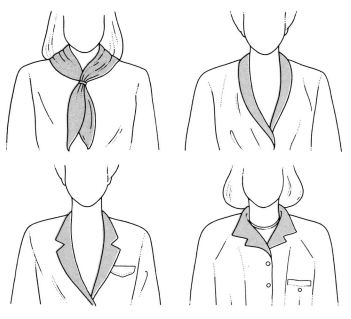

Raglan sleeves play down wide shoulders.

BOTTOM LEFT
Shoulder padding widens narrow shoulders.

THE SHOULDERS

Neck size is, of course, proportionate to shoulder size, and a narrow neck will look even narrower if it is supported by excessively padded, square shoulders. With padded shoulders your waist and hips look narrower in contrast and profit by comparison. Padded shoulders help to create an inverted triangle silhouette shape. With the hips *appearing* to be narrower than the shoulders – because the latter have been widened by contouring either with pads or styling – thick waists, hips and thighs become streamlined. By accentuating the shoulders, a designer draws the observer's eyes upwards to the head and face.

For women with narrow or sloping shoulders, this can prove a difficult balance to achieve. Extra padding in the shoulders will build up the shoulderline in garments such as jackets and coats, but you should avoid emphasis there – with heavy detail like epaulettes, for instance.

Wide shoulders have been an asset in many modern fashion shapes, although beware of cut-away halter necks if you are bony. Wide shoulders could be a problem too if we ever see a return to Empire lines and the demure softness of the Regency period, the look of a Jane Austen heroine, with those swan-like shoulders. Sleeves that are 'set in', as in fully fashioned knitwear, can make the shoulders look more narrow and rounded.

YOO HOO MR. ARMITAGE..

THE ARMS

If you have flabby arms, then you might choose to keep them covered, with a sleeve to the elbow. In fact, even at the peak of summer, I would suggest it is advisable to wear some sort of sleeve at work, as bare arms look too casual in the office. Cap sleeves, or sleeves to the elbow are most flattering. Any sleeve that stops shorter than the elbow will create a line that cuts across the upper arm and draw the eyes to it. Short arms will be further shortened by the lines of sleeves cutting across them, or a lot of cuff detail. Long arms that can seem gangly can benefit from this. (But cuff detail will draw attention to your hands.)

Covering the arms in very full puffed sleeves will broaden the shape of the upper part of the body. Sleeves that are wide at the cuffline give a rather floppy look and are not particularly practical, unless easily rolled.

Always make sure that jacket sleeves are the right length for your arms: sleeves should stop at the wrist-bone, or a little shorter if you want to show bangles and bracelets. The right sleeve length for you personally is essential to the way a jacket looks. Consider this a priority when having any alterations done to a new jacket.

THE BUST

A short sleeve that ends near the bustline will draw attention to a large bust, and create a horizontal line right across the top half of the body. Collars, ruffles, breast pockets, cluttered necklines and chokers will all draw attention to the bust. Drape yourself in fabrics that are not too bulky, in simple, well-fitting styles. Avoid clingy materials, and remember that tight vertical lines are a disaster! Crossover styles and square necklines work well in that the shapes of the lines draw the eye vertically upwards rather than across. Above all, buy clothes that are cut large enough – there is nothing worse than gaping buttonholes!

Small busts are best camouflaged by blouses or jackets that have pockets over the bustline, or that are gathered on the yoke from the shoulderline, falling softly over the bust. Dresses that show a lot of cleavage should be avoided. If you want a lower neckline, then go for a top that crosses over the bust with lots of soft folds. Avoid skirts and trousers which make your bottom half seem larger in comparison with your top half. Full skirts and baggy trousers will create a further imbalance.

THE WAIST

Small waists can be emphasized by wearing thick belts. If your hips are by contrast a lot larger than your waist, then always buy skirts with belt loops, and the belt can take up some of the slack fabric around the waist. You will have plenty of room to

TOP LEFT
Cluttered necklines will draw attention to a large bust, and should be avoided.

TOP RIGHT
Large busts will look best in simple, well-fitting styles with clean lines.

MIDDLE LEFT
Tightly fitting tops and full skirts should be avoided by those with small busts, as they make the lower half of the body seem heavier.

MIDDLE RIGHT
A small bustline is flattered by a fuller top which is softly gathered and does not cling.

BOTTOM LEFT
Those with thick waists should avoid waisted clothes and belts which emphasize this problem area.

BOTTOM RIGHT
Tops that finish well below the waistline and belts worn on the hips will help to draw attention away from thick waists.

tuck your sweater inside your skirt, even after you have had a good alteration done.

Thick waists need not be accentuated. Avoid waisted clothes (drawing lines across the body, therefore shortening it) and opt instead for clothes that fall from the shoulder to a narrow hemline. If the garment has a belt, or different sections, they should join at your hips or below. Remember detail and seams draw attention to an area, so use them to emphasize those dimensions that you like.

If you are short waisted, fitted clothes are likely to require major alterations. You are wiser choosing clothes with less structure on the top half of the body. Long waisted women should be careful when buying garments with waistlines that the waist is not cutting into their midriff; they might be wiser to look for outfits that are drop waisted or completely *un*waisted.

THE HIPS AND THIGHS

Wide hips and large bottoms are aspects of the traditional 'pear shape'. They can be given less emphasis by proportionately building up the top half of the body. Shoulder pads, lighter colours and denser, patterned or textured fabrics will draw the eye upwards. Thick thighs should not be sheathed in clinging fabric, and billowing bell shapes worn with close fitting tops will only reinforce a 'bottom heavy' impression. It is a common mistake to think that wide hips and a large bottom can be disguised by wearing full skirts, or A-line skirts. A straight narrow skirt could seem to emphasize the problem areas. However, if the straight skirt is well cut and is worn with a square-shouldered top, then the problem areas will seem narrower. Anything that pulls the eye downwards – details like pockets on the hips, large check trousers, drop waistlines – will emphasize bottoms and hips. Shirts, tunics and jackets that cover these areas are a godsend! A straight skirt on a fuller figure fits and looks better if it has a couple of pleats at the waistline: these pleats must fold *outwards* to camouflage the stomach and to give a sleek appearance (folding inwards they look very rounded when viewed from the side). This is also a good tip for fuller-figured men and their trousers.

THE LEGS

Very thin legs or large calves with tiny ankles will look better in a longer skirt. Be aware that your hemline is creating a horizontal line across the leg and will therefore again draw attention to that part of the leg. If you hate your knees, then a hemline that stops just short of them will only add further emphasis. Similarly, thin legs under a very full skirt will look even thinner (make them look less so by wearing textured hosiery).

'There is no excellent beauty that hath not some strangeness in the proportion!'
Sir Francis Bacon,
Philosopher (1561-1626)

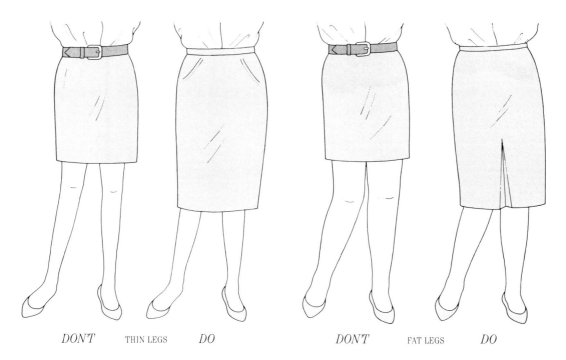

DON'T   THIN LEGS   *DO*   *DON'T*   FAT LEGS   *DO*

A far more common problem is fat legs. Often, when a woman has lost a lot of weight, there is one area where the fat stubbornly remains – her legs. Very dainty shoes will only emphasize their chunkiness, and narrow skirts with hemline detail – pleats, for example – will draw further attention to them. Black tights (especially in Lycra), when appropriate with the rest of the outfit, are very flattering for podgy pins! In fact, to create as sleek a line as possible, it's a good idea to match shoe and tight colour. This will make the leg look longer. Darker shades will make the leg look slimmer; lighter colours and bold patterns will make the legs look prominent.

Remember short skirts need good legs or legs that can be camouflaged with hosiery that is flattering.

Never give up on yourself just because you've large hips or a big bust, and garments never seem to fit you properly. You are in the majority in not fitting a standard size perfectly. You could well be restricting yourself, out of force of habit, to certain shapes. Be adventurous. Experiment with many different shapes, and you could get a pleasant surprise. Eventually, you will forget about the bust or bottom that has been such a problem, and with the confidence that good camouflage and re-emphasis brings, you can take a renewed – and quite justifiable – pride in your appearance!

'Woman is fine for her own satisfaction alone; man only knows man's insensibility to a new gown.'
Jane Austen
Novelist (1775-1817)

COLOUR AND COLOURING

You should choose the colours of your clothes to enhance your own colouring. However, having said this, I believe that any woman can wear any colour as long as it is accessorized properly. I think it is unnecessary and boring to restrict yourself to certain colours, especially as the texture of a cloth so affects its colour: a cold blue in a cotton or silk can look much softer and warmer in, say, cashmere or wool.

Colours can be warm and cold, deep and light, muted or clear, and within every colour are extensive ranges of tones. We tend to have either blue or yellow tones predominating in our colouring, and hair, skin or eye colour will often have a tendency to suggest one colour more strongly than the other. You can often tell which tones predominate by looking at the iris of the eye – it will have blue or yellow flecks in it. Your hair, too, will have either golden or reddish lights.

Most cosmetic houses and counters in department stores will tell you which tone you are. Estée Lauder's Prescriptives' whole philosophy is based on the blue/yellow concept, for example. However, a quicker way is to try on a pink and an orange lipstick to see which looks better on you (ask some friends' for their opinions too). If the pink one suits you, you're tending towards the blue tone – and you can guess the alternative!

Very roughly, a blue-toned skin is the 'English rose', pinky, fair complexion; a yellow-toned skin is more olive or sallow, perhaps Mediterranean in colouring. Some women have a mixture of both tones – how lucky they are, as are those with black skins. They look fantastic in everything!

It is easy to take for granted your piercing green or blue eyes, or the deep red glints in your hair, but picking out these colours in the clothes you wear will enhance your best features. A woman with dramatic colouring – black hair and pale blue eyes, for example – can wear more dramatic colours than a sandy-haired woman with pale skin and freckles. Her colours should play up to the delicacy and warmth of her colouring.

Avoid making drastic changes in your colouring either through hair chemicals or make-up. A brunette who longs to be blonde will look very harsh if she lightens her hair dramatically. If your skin does not tan easily then a strong fake tan either through lotion or make-up will look incongruous. (Increased knowledge about the connection between the sun and skin cancer and ageing has lessened the kudos of the sun-tan anyway.)

Skin and hair tend to lose their depth of colour and fade as women get older, and they could find that colours that have suited them all their lives may need changing. That's not to say that older women can't wear bright colours any more, they might choose the same colours, but in softer fabrics once they

'It's important to look neat and tidy and not be too flashily dressed. If you look untidy you're considered to have an untidy mind – it's as simple as that!

Lynda Chalker
MP quoted in *Flying High*

reach their sixties. And as far as hair is concerned, an older woman who darkens it will tend to look harsh and 'washed out' if she is not careful.

Many of the effects of colour, both on ourselves and how others perceive us wearing certain colours, are to do with reflection of light. Black, always a fashion colour however hard fashion trends try to persuade us otherwise, reflects very little light. If you have very delicate colouring you could look drained in black, as it provides such a strong contrast to your face. Also, worn near the face, black can drain light from it. Compensate by wearing light-reflecting jewellery – silver, gold and especially pearls in earrings and necklaces around the face. You should sport a bright lipstick to bring life and colour to the face and prevent your features being overpowered. You may not realize it, but different foundations reflect different degrees of light; a more luminous foundation as opposed to a very matt one might brighten your complexion, as will blusher.

Some colours are difficult to wear because they pick up bad points in your colouring. Navy, for instance, can often make you look tired, because it picks up the 'blueness' in shadows under the eyes. You should counteract this by making sure that the shadows are adequately covered, and by wearing a clear bright lipstick that attracts the eye. Khakis, browns and beiges can also make you look drained when worn near the face. These are muted shades and are best worn by those with warm clear colouring. Golden-skinned honey blondes look good in these shades, as do some redheads. If you are in doubt about these colours, whites and creams, with their strong reflective qualities, are almost certain to be flattering. White and cream look crisp and clean worn near the face, 'lifting' the features and reflecting light on to them.

Your colouring is affected by the seasons, in that you are paler in the autumn and winter than in summer and spring. Also there is less sunlight in the winter months and the light itself seems much harsher. If you tan easily, then at the height of summer you could look terrific in black wearing very little make-up; in the winter months you all need to wear more make-up to add some colour to your face. As the tendency is to wear darker colours in winter, accordingly you need stronger make-up in order not to look washed-out. You can always add light warm colour to the face by wearing a jewel-bright scarf with that dark overcoat. The chart on page 45 gives you some idea of how you can vary colours worn with your basic neutrals in winter and summer.

Lighting is different at different times of day, and in the evening it is dimmer which means stronger make-up, and deeper colours; light-reflecting surfaces such as glitter and sequins, satin and silk will look appropriate (in the stronger light of daytime they would look garish). This difference in

'Good clothes open all doors.'
Thomas Fuller,
English writer (1608-61)

lighting should always be considered when choosing evening wear. If you are dying to wear bright colours, then the evening might be a better time to wear them.

In terms of the working wardrobe, I always advise customers to use bright or strong colours in moderation. This is because particular bright shades (which come into fashion once every five or six seasons) can date very quickly. Retailers tend to be very cautious when buying bright colours because of this. They are not always appropriate for business dress anyway, because they have connotations and associations which perhaps say 'too much' about the wearer. So use bright colour in your shirt, the equivalent of the man's tie, if you like colour, and choose shades that enhance your colouring.

Bright colour used in large blocks looks garish and unflattering – a pair of canary yellow trousers is going to attract attention to your lower body and detract from your face and what you are saying. Bright colours throughout an outfit can overpower your personality and make you look as though you need to attract attention at a very superficial level by the way you dress.

So choose large items such as suits, coats and jackets in neutrals – the blacks, browns, beiges, taupes, creams and greys. The advantages of neutrals are clear because, unless they are very pale, they do not dirty easily; they do not on the whole need careful matching; you do not tire of them in the way that you tire of a bright colour; they do not date; and other people rarely find them offensive, in the way that someone might really dislike green as a colour for example.

Interest can always be created in neutrals by the texture of the material or by flecks of colour in the weave. Indeed, neutrals can be in patterns – like checks – and when I specify a colour, it can be a *pattern*. Don't mix patterns too much though; that's quite difficult to do successfully.

Bolder flashes of colour – a red scarf with camel, or a peach blouse with grey – can stop neutrals being dull. Accessories help too: chunky silver earrings can dramatize that grey knitted suit, and a tortoiseshell necklace will bring life to a cream blouse. I always think it a shame when women tell me that they think neutrals are boring: they've obviously been looking at the wrong sort of neutrals in the wrong sort of shops and don't know how to individualize them.

There is increasing interest in the significance of colour and in colour psychology. Certainly, in the most basic sense, some colours *do* seem to have an uplifting effect, and others the reverse. I believe that an open mind and a willingness to experiment with colour will soon teach you what suits you best and what you feel happiest in. The following rough guidelines should help you choose colours for your skin and hair colouring with flair and confidence.

A TORTOISESHELL NECKLACE WILL BRING LIFE TO A CREAM BLOUSE.

Rough Colouring Tone Guidelines

This chart is designed to show how neutrals can look different at various times of the year. The quality of daylight changes from summer to winter, and what can look crisp and fresh in the summer – a plain white blouse, for instance – can appear harsh and unflattering under winter's glare. And in winter, we get paler too.

In summer, navy worn with white can be a most dynamic combination; in winter, navy looks better worn with a warmth-bringing tan or gold. Red worn with black in the summer could look heavy; it is better to combine the black with a lighter colour such as lemon.

In winter, pure white can be difficult to wear as it tends to provide a stark contrast with any other shade. If one of my

Accent Colour Guidelines

Within each shirt or colour suggested, look for the blue or yellow tones, and choose accordingly.

Colour of Basic Garment, e.g. Suit	Shirts or Sweaters	
	Winter	Summer
Black	Ivory	White
	Red	Hyacinth Blue
	Beige	Khaki
	Khaki	Lemon
	Tan	Tan
White	Ivory	White
		Cream
		Peach
		Pearl/Grey
		Khaki
Navy	Gold	Khaki
	Tan	Chartreuse
		Tan
		Coral
		White
Taupe	Black	White
	Old Rose	
	Ivory	
Camel	Black	White
	Navy	
	Brown	
Grey	Black	White
	Red	Peach
	Cream	Aqua
		Coral

customers wants to wear white wool in winter, then I suggest she mixes it with other 'winter white' clothes. Winter white usually has a more creamy tone to it and looks ivory because it is made in thicker fibres giving a softer impression.

Green In every green, there is either a blue base or a yellow base, and if you look carefully you will be able to recognize this. A forest green, for instance, has blue undertones; a lime green, yellow.

Red Brick reds and pillarbox reds have yellow undertones; cherry reds and burgundy reds have blue undertones. There are also browny reds which are better for those who are yellow toned, as browns and yellows are very similar.

Blue/Purple A yellow-toned person could wear aqua blue, but couldn't necessarily wear the royal blue of the blue-toned person (except when they were tanned, of course). Purple is a blue-toned colour.

Yellow/Orange A blue-toned person would look better in softer ochres rather than citric colours, whereas a woman with yellow-toned skin would look lovely in a bright buttercup yellow. Yellow is probably one of the more difficult colours for someone with a blue-toned skin, but if they wore more subdued tones, like buttermilk, they could probably get away with it.

Pink The yellow-toned woman has difficulty here as I've already mentioned, but she could wear peach. Fuchsia is marvellous on a blue-toned skin, as well as pastel pinks.

Camel Certain camels are very yellowy and come much more into the tan category. The more stoney creams would be better for a blue-toned skin.

Brown Dark, bitter chocolate brown has bluey-grey undertones, so will look better on a blue-toned skin, as would a taupe, which has a pink undertone. A tan or reddish brown would be better on yellow tones.

Black/White There can be no hard and fast rules with these two, as they're such special colours, and it's all very individualistic. A lighter skin wears black better; an olive skin can look terrible in black. If you want to wear white, wear an off-white or ivory because it is kinder to all skins. Stark white tends to look hard, unless it is in linen or cotton.

Grey Grey has a lot of blue undertones in it, and fair-skinned blondes look wonderful in grey. Darker people don't look particularly good in it. I personally wouldn't wear grey unless it had some sort of relief design – like white fleck – or I would accessorize with colour, otherwise I'd look drawn and tired.

'I have a hatred of being a feminine version of a man. You can wear perfectly ordinary, feminine clothes. Pinstripes and lapels do not make you any better at your job.'

Jennifer D'Abo
then Chairman, Ryman plc

CHAPTER FIVE

EVALUATING YOUR PRESENT WARDROBE

O nce you've 'evaluated' yourself, so to speak, you're well on the way towards a major reappraisal of the clothes hanging in your wardrobe. You should now know what you should be looking for in terms of cut, cloth and colour, what suits you and what doesn't, and what is appropriate to your colouring.

LIFESTYLES

There is yet another consideration. For, just as you previously took a thorough look at yourself – at your size, proportion and colouring – so you now need to look at the life that you lead. If you have a very clear idea of how you need to dress for the various activities in your life, as well as what best suits you, then you are unlikely to succumb to impulse buying and will be more able to 'prune' your existing wardrobe intelligently. For many wardrobes can be bulging with a large selection of clothes, bought over a number of years – and perhaps even encompassing a few 'lifestyles' – and yet their owner can never find the right clothes to wear. If this is so, then the wardrobe is definitely not in harmony with your current lifestyle and the time has come for reappraisal. Many women never ask themselves 'What do I need for the life that I lead?', and I am convinced that this is a prime consideration in making the very best of your appearance.

Ask yourself what percentage of your life you spend working, socializing or at leisure. For most of us, the first one is the category requiring most thought, and the one which concerns us most in this book.

Practical considerations are of prime importance. Does your work involve travelling, either on a daily basis or on longer

'Some mornings I have to put the right clothes on to be the person I have to be at work – clothes almost act as "armour".
I think that the clients I work with over a long period look forward to seeing what I'm going to wear – when they first see me in the morning they think "Oh, she's in that frame of mind this morning."'

Penny Jones,
Management Consultant
and Psychologist

trips? If you use public transport daily, then you will be exposed to the elements, and warmth and keeping dry will be priorities. If you spend a lot of time in your car, then 'creasability' will be a factor. If you go on longer trips, all of these elements will apply, but 'packability' and versatility will be vital too (see Chapter Ten).

If your working day involves much walking, or standing around, then your choice of footwear should account for this. Perhaps you have to be 'on site' as an architect, or wear an overall as a doctor. Bear in mind the amount of physical activity your job entails, too: if you are rushing from one appointment to another, then mobility and comfort will be important. A job like teaching could mean that your clothes need to be cleaned easily, what with dirty little fingers and chalk dust! The temperature of your working environment – the extent to which it is heated and air-conditioned – will also matter, and this will determine the weight of fabric that you choose.

Depending on the type of work that you do, some of your socializing could be work-related. If you conduct business over lunch or dinner then your clothes will need to be 'dressed up' or versatile enough that they can take you through the day. You may have little call to dress formally, however, when socializing away from work. But if your husband does a lot of socializing that is work-related, perhaps you may have to accompany him or entertain on his behalf. If he is working in a business that is very different from yours, and where people present themselves very differently, then you might choose to adapt the image that you present accordingly. (Of course, by choosing *not* to do so, you can make a clear and bold statement about your own independence – but this might not be too wise!)

Bear in mind what you do on your return from work. If you charge straight into the kitchen to start cooking, then a large protective apron is an essential investment! And if you're a working mother, you'll need clothes that can easily be cleaned and allow greater mobility (cotton jersey is a safe bet here). If you look smart all day at work in formal clothes, then flopping in a tracksuit at the end of a long day really helps the mental 'wind-down'.

'Image', too, is important when considering lifestyle, and evaluating your wardrobe. Consider the particular demands of your role at work in terms of what you and your clothes want or need to say. If you are in a profession where people come to you for advice – maybe accountancy, law or medicine – then you will need to look dependable, trustworthy and reassuring. This can be done with your clothes. If you are in a job where you have to exert authority, then dressing to command respect will help. A more obviously creative business like advertising or publishing will create different demands; you will want to express your creativity and ability to think originally through

'Male city colleagues often appreciate when you've made an effort with your clothes. But don't expect them to appreciate the real problems women face in deciding how to dress for work.'

Jane Cooper,
Senior Manager, Banking

your clothes. It is also worthy considering the variety of people you deal with at work and their sets of values. A designer working with other designers will probably feel free to dress with creativity and originality, both qualities which are admired by her peer group. A creative director of an advertising agency, however, could well have to meet fairly conservative clients, and her appearance will need to be adaptable.

'Image' consultants are often used as advisers in this area, but sometimes the advice given stems from rigid ideas that do not take the person's individuality into consideration. Of course when we look at ourselves in the mirror, we do so completely subjectively and our current level of self-esteem informs the judgements. This is where impartial advice can be so useful, and at Wardrobe we are committed to researching the customers' background, their roles and the demands of their lifestyles, so that we can suggest clothes that are entirely appropriate for *their* needs, rather than anyone else's requirements.

WARDROBE REAPPRAISAL

Changes in your life may mean that you need to reorganize and revitalize your wardrobe. If you are starting a new job or your own business, are getting married or divorced, then you may well wish to present yourself in a new light. Promotion can mean that you are far more in the public eye than you were before. Gaining or losing a lot of weight will mean that some clothes no longer fit you properly. You might be one of those women (and you are not in a minority!) who possess clothes ranging from a size 10 to a 14, catering for fluctuations in your weight. Take this opportunity to discard that fantasy of ever being a size 10 again, and resolve from now on to make the very best of your size 12 or 14 frame through skilled clothes shopping. You might want to reorganize your wardrobe as part of a new resolution to be more organized generally, or you could be moving house and rationalizing all your possessions, your wardrobe included.

If you have spent years buying clothes without 'scheme or analysis' or detailed planning, then examining your wardrobe can be a chastening experience. You are likely to discover that you have a lot of clothes that do not work particularly well together. Impulse buys, strong fashion fads in style or material (for example, large shapeless Japanese clothes) or clothes in shades that do not blend in with the rest of your wardrobe, should be discarded. Do not feel guilty – you are going to make your life more efficient by having a well-managed wardrobe.

It is important to mention here, I think, that possessing a large number of clothes has little bearing on presenting yourself well, and that a woman who dresses with style does not need to wear something different to work every day. Obviously you want range and versatility in your clothes, but this comes as much from their quality in the broadest sense of the word, as from their quantity. (My 'less is more' theory.)

Before you start to sift through your clothes, arm yourself with paper and pen and a full-length mirror in good light. We never go grocery shopping without first checking what we have in stock; incredibly we never seem to do this when going shopping for clothes, and yet the financial outlay is far greater. If you draw up a wardrobe 'list' – a guide to everything that's in your existing wardrobe – and take it with you (either physically or mentally) when you go shopping, it will help enormously. Your description of your clothes should follow the basic 'cut, cloth, colour' guidelines – for example, 'one straight skirt with side pleat, black wool'. This is to make sure that you get the proportion of your future purchases correct, with the cut and the density of the cloth chosen to complement the garment you are trying to match. For further information see the next chapter.

Give yourself plenty of time to do this reappraisal. If you are in a rush, then you could well throw out clothes impulsively, and later regret it. You need time to consider what exactly suits you and why you feel comfortable in it.

'I used to have far too many clothes, although I always complained that I had nothing to wear! A large amount of time and money was spent on clothes, which would then be taken home, hung up and rarely worn. I had no idea what clothes I owned, because too many of them in the wardrobe couldn't be seen.'

Stephanie Ellis,
Civil Servant

WEEDING OUT

First of all, pick out clothes that you are especially fond of and wear a lot. Why do you like them? Have people told you that the colour particularly suits you? Does the fit feel good, the cut flatter your figure? Is the cloth practical in the way it can be cleaned, and the extent to which it creases? Some clothes in this category will defy analysis and be garments that you feel an emotional attachment for. If they are redolent of affectionate memories, I suggest that you hang on to them – they are, after all, a part of your history.

Whilst sifting through these 'old favourites', it is worth checking their condition – do they need hems repairing, buttons replacing, or cleaning? Make a note of these details. They're all part of your appearance, and of the 'messages' you send to people around you. Check too, that these 'old favourites' have not gone under the arms, or that skirts and trousers have not lost their shape by bagging at the knees and seat. If they have, then accept that they are past redemption.

And I'd advise you to include lingerie and jewellery in this overhaul. Because jewellery takes up so little space, it is easy to hoard, and this can make it difficult to choose the right pieces quickly for the outfit that you are wearing. As for lingerie and tights, there is nothing more infuriating than putting on pair after pair of tights in the morning to find that they are all laddered – then when you do find a pair that is intact, your haste causes you to ladder them as you tug them on! Most of us have a weakness for a type of accessory: some women are 'baga-holics', others love shoes, and some own dozens of belts. Now's the time to acknowledge this fetish and somewhat rationalize it! Work out just how often you've worn an accessory and whether this warrants it remaining in your wardrobe.

Now let's look at clothes that you no longer wear, or were obvious mistakes. If you've not worn an item for two years or more, then it probably has no place in your wardrobe. Anything that does not fit properly and cannot be altered, that has an exaggerated, out-of-date cut (shorter boxy jackets, for instance, which will only go with a small number of bottom halves, or clothes with exaggerated fashion detail such as appliqué, embroidery or epaulettes), or that is in a colour popular a couple of seasons ago (greens, purples and pinks, in particular, date very rapidly), should be discarded. It will be hard, but it's got to be done!

Fashion is cyclical, which might tempt you to keep certain garments 'until they come back in'. No fashion design is entirely original because fashion, like art, is derivative. Inno-vative fashion design is a new interpretation of what has gone before, a different way of using cut, cloth or colour. You could take a modern 1980s jacket and find it has a great deal in common with one from the 1940s: they could both be fairly fitted, with padded shoulders, and fully lined. However, in the decades between the jackets, fabric manufacture, cloth cutting and dyeing have all become far more sophisticated. So, although your immediate response could be that the jackets look very similar, technological development has meant that they are, in fact, two quite different garments.

The fashion industry also needs to protect itself. A trend might re-emerge three or four years after it made its first appearance, but it will always be modified. The short skirts in fashion at the time of writing are far 'curvier' in their construc-tion than the pelmet-like minis of the Sixties. Of course, the fashion world is not always successful in dictating to us what to wear (midi-skirts in the Seventies were a disaster), and neither should it be. Clothes need to meet the requirements of *real* women, who work and run homes. (But I hope that, by now, if any of you are secretly hoarding bell-bottomed jeans, then I've persuaded you to throw them out!)

If the cut of a garment looks dated, then it is likely to be cut on the small side. In this decade, with the exception of body-skimming styles in stretchy fabrics, a larger cut has been estab-lished, in tailored clothes as well. Sweaters and blouses, which rarely date, will look old-fashioned now with narrowly cut shoulders, even if the body shape is narrower to match.

You could be uncertain about some clothes, because you

think that they might fit into your wardrobe but you are not certain how. Scarves, handkerchieves and squares of material can be very useful here. A customer of mine, for instance, wanted a top to go with a green pleated silk skirt. She loved a white jacket that we had in stock, but she did not think that it complemented her skirt. I suggested that she buy a square of patterned silk which included white and the green of her skirt in its colours, and wear it in the breast pocket of the jacket. Immediately, she looked smart and coordinated, and no-one would have thought that the skirt and jacket were mismatched. So try and view afresh the way you combine your clothes – sometimes an older garment can take on a new lease of life being worn in a different colour combination and with new accessories.

A plain blouse, for instance, can be jazzed up by changing the buttons – adding pearl or metal ones, maybe. Jackets, coats, sweaters, blouses and dresses can all be updated by adding shoulder pads to create a more contemporary line. A belt will make something shapeless look more fitted. If shorter skirts are fashionable then you can get hems shortened. You might need to taper the side seams when shortening a skirt if it was originally quite long. (Any alterations, unless you are a skilled seamstress, are best done professionally, though.) If you are keen to update your clothes, yet short of money, then I'd advise you to visit the haberdashery department of a large store to seek inspiration from the possibilities of squares of fabric, buttons and shoulder pads.

You might want to sell the clothes that you no longer want, or give them to a younger relative or a charity shop. If you discover that a large number of your clothes are redundant, do not get disheartened. Analyse what was wrong about their cut, cloth and colour, resolve not to make those mistakes again, and to buy high-fashion garments with discretion in the future.

'Good items never die.'
Ralph Lauren,
Fashion designer

BUILDING ON WHAT'S LEFT

Even if you have been buying clothes in the most whimsical, arbitrary way, some colour should predominate. You would be well-advised to make the most predominant neutral the base colour in your new wardrobe. That is not as restricting as it sounds, as groups of neutrals are highly compatible – taupes, creams, tans, camels and browns mix well together, as do blacks and greys.

Using neutrals as the basis for your wardrobe need not mean that you will end up looking dull and colourless. If you chose navy as a predominant neutral, you could also choose khaki which is a complete contrast. The two colours look good together, and both separately look very smart with splashes of red, for example.

Always take your colouring into consideration when choosing neutrals. A woman whose colouring is yellow based, for instance, will not look as good as she could if all her neutral basics are in cold colours.

To create cohesion with what you already have in your wardrobe, I suggest you take two items which you like and wear frequently – a brown skirt and a grey skirt for instance. To pull your wardrobe together, the first purchase you should make should be a jacket, preferably checked or patterned with black and brown in it. According to which neutral you favour as a base for your wardrobe, that colour can predominate in your jacket. Assuming you own sweaters or blouses that go with the skirts, you already now have two smart outfits for business. Season by season you can develop this wardrobe by adding trousers, sweaters, shirts and dresses, all of which blend with the jacket. A well-chosen jacket can revive the most exhausted wardrobe.

Perhaps you already have enough tailored clothes, but your wardrobe still seems jaded and dull. Sometimes you might not be getting enough wear out of a jacket or skirt because you do not have the right blouse to go with it. As a change from tailored lines, a knitted suit, in cotton or wool, looks smart and feels comfortable for work. It is handy, of course, to have a jacket that could go over it if needed.

If you are developing a new wardrobe, do not choose a radically different style from the one you had before, unless you are absolutely sure that it is a style you are comfortable with. Planning your wardrobe from the basis of a jacket or a suit, you should only need to make one or two major purchases per season.

If colour matches are difficult then always take clothes that you want to match along to the shops, and check in natural light. Working within a group of colours, you will soon train your eye to spot colours that fit in within your spectrum.

In the following chapter we will examine more fully how to develop a flexible and coordinated wardrobe.

CHAPTER SIX

THE CAPSULE WORKING WARDROBE

What I am advocating in this chapter – and throughout the book – is that you eventually *reduce* the number of clothes in your wardrobe rather than *increase* them. Instead of owning lots of clothes, many of which are not worn much, I'd like to help you own a smaller number of clothes from which you get greater wear – my 'less is more' theory. The capsule working wardrobe, therefore, is a small, considered collection of clothes providing an effective minimum number of garments to meet your daily needs. It is the solid foundation upon which to build the rest of your wardrobe. The 'capsule' centres on a jacket and includes a skirt – or a suit – trousers, blouse, sweater, dresses, coat and raincoat and evening wear. These individual components will work well together if they are chosen wisely and with forethought, and will provide an outfit for every occasion. You should never again have to face the dilemma of 'what on earth shall I wear!'

The first thing to consider – whether you are starting from scratch, or basing your capsule on a thoroughly edited or weeded-out existing wardrobe – is your budget. I am often asked what percentage of earnings a woman should spend on her clothes. There is no definitive answer, as it all depends on individual priorities. If expensive foreign holidays or an impressive car are important, then you might need to economize on clothes – not a priority *I* should choose, of course!

I would always advise you to go for *good* clothes – and these are never cheap – although I must emphasize that it doesn't follow that all expensive clothes are necessarily good. If the best cloth is used for the best clothes, this will hang beautifully and wear extremely well; as it will have cost the designer a great deal per metre before it is even made up, much of the eventual cost of the garment is incurred early on in the

OPPOSITE PAGE
A classic suit can be split up and the jacket worn with different bottom halves – a dependable basis for your capsule wardrobe.

— 54 —

manufacturing process. As well as good cloth, the cut or design of the garment is all important too, and a 'name' – which will add again to the cost – will ensure a lasting appeal if it is in a classic rather than high fashion style.

Classics are clothes that have extended lifespans. In the case of classic leisurewear – Aran, Guernsey or Shetland sweaters, say – they are clothes that are eminently practical and functional, and which were originally worn as such by people of certain cultures and ways of life. They are clothes that are not blatantly 'of this day'. However, as fashions change, certain items become classics because of their wearability. These modern classics show the influence of recent decades, and so the very best aspects of fashion are preserved through their popularity. Denim jeans, which were originally worn by gold prospectors, and popularized during the 1950s, are as loved today as they were then. They are definitely a modern classic.

Traditional classic clothes – such as cashmere jumpers and Burberry raincoats – have remained the same for decades. They are clothes that suit a large number of people, are very comfortable, and do not date. This does not mean that they are boring, though; a classic cut in an unusual cloth need never look 'safe' dressing. Because of their long life, classics tend to be expensive and come in neutral colours – such as blacks, creams, browns and navies – and designers of classic clothes are usually well-established with a loyal following (understandable when you consider the enduring nature of their designs). However, a wardrobe composed entirely of classics is likely to be predictable, especially if they are all traditional classics, and I shall outline some variations and combinations in the individual sections following. Besides which, however much you dislike shopping, the prospect of not needing to buy anything for several years is a stultifying one for most women!

So, good clothes, and a proportion of classic clothes, are vital in any working woman's wardrobe, and I cannot emphasize too strongly how important I consider this. For, because of and despite the initial high cost, the 'cost-per-wear' of the clothes is considerably lessened. Simply explained, if a garment costs £150 and you wear it many times (because it continually looks good and wears well), it costs you next to nothing each time. On the other hand, an impulse bargain that you wear once costs you exactly what you paid for it, a pretty expensive showing! When buying clothes, particularly major purchases, always ask yourself 'How often will I wear it?' It could be that a garment you are unsure whether to buy because of the cost, will turn out to be a very worthwhile and sensible investment. The amount you pay for your clothes should always be determined by their 'wearability' – and the pleasure you think you'll get from wearing them.

'I'm convinced that the subject of executive dressing is not frivolous. I can't be alone in feeling and acting more assertively when well dressed. For years I believed my brains would bring me all the success I wanted; but recently I've begun to realize that nice clothes help with confidence at work...'

Katharine Whitehorn,
Journalist, writing in *The Observer*

THE JACKET

The jacket is likely to be the most useful garment in your capsule wardrobe and, if you choose wisely, an investment from which you will get a great deal of wear. If you are going to splash out on one garment to revitalize your wardrobe, then a jacket will show a high 'cost-per-wear' return, and is your wisest starting point.

I always advocate wearing a jacket to meetings, presentations and interviews. A tailored jacket is acceptable business dress to everyone at all levels. If you have an impromptu important meeting, throw on your jacket and you'll instantly look the part. Have you ever seen a man go into a meeting in shirtsleeves?

Clean uncluttered lines are best, and simple shapes. You want to create a shape that is approximately an inverted triangle. If you are on a budget, avoid very strong fashion influences like wide lapels, and anything extremely baggy or close fitting. You do not want to buy a jacket that dates quickly or lacks versatility.

Double-breasted jackets can be slimming because they have a parallel pair of lines (created by the margin and two rows of buttons), drawing the eye vertically. However, if you have a large bust and do not wish to draw attention to it, then these parallel lines will emphasize it. A longer single-breasted jacket would be a wiser choice for you.

If you are concerned about looking severe in a jacket then choose one which has rounded rather than square shoulders, and a rounder cut of lapel. A collarless jacket, worn with an appropriate garment underneath, can have a softening effect on a woman who feels that she has a tendency to look 'strict'.

The traditional classic jacket is a double-breasted, set-in sleeve blazer, made in navy or beige cashmere. It is not as long as many of today's jackets and rose to popularity in the mid 1970s. The modern classic version of this is a longer jacket, more fitted at the waist, with softly rounded, but still padded, shoulders. Cheaper jackets tend to button higher up, and a skimpy cut will not allow for movement in the upper part of the garment, therefore they can be difficult to work in. Very short jackets tend to date quickly and can be a nightmare to match up with lower halves because the two different cuts may not be compatible. It is better to buy shorter jackets as part of a suit.

A jacket should not be too tight across the back or it will restrict movement in the shoulders and arms. The armholes should be roomy enough to wear a fine sweater underneath, allow room for movement and not constrict, causing risk of soiling by perspiration. Check that the sleeves allow scope for elbow movement – I always advise moving around in the jacket when trying it on.

The cut and fabric of a jacket should complement one

'You see a man, the lowest stock clerk, and he will have on a jacket; and you see a woman in a clerical position and she looks as if she is dressed to take out the garbage or the laundry.'

Leah Hertz,
from The Business
Amazons

another. Bulky materials such as tweed are going to create substantial seams, so they work better in boxier shapes. A shape that is more moulded to the body will work better in a more fluid material, like a light-weight wool. One of the problems with buying cheaper versions of designer jackets is that very often the manufacturer will use a cheaper fabric and therefore the cut and the cloth will not be compatible, and the jacket will not hang well.

The price of a jacket is usually determined by the price of the cloth, the detail of the cut, and the quality of dye used in the colour. Practical considerations such as the temperature in which you work, and how often the jacket will need cleaning affect the choice of cloth. A 'cool wool' or 'summer wool' (similar material to most men's light-weight suiting) is very versatile and can be worn almost all the year round, depending on what you put underneath it. (If you're keen to build up a fully comprehensive wardrobe, then you could aim to buy two medium-weight jackets in, say, cool wool or gaberdine, one heavy-weight jacket in a heavy wool or tweed, and one light-weight jacket in a linen or cotton.)

A patterned or textured cloth will be the most versatile and, provided the detail is subtle, less tiring on the eye than a block of solid colour. The success of the capsule wardrobe depends very much on the choice of jacket cloth. It should be chosen to fit in with several 'bottom halves': skirts and trousers. The pattern need not be obtrusive. Discreet patterns, small checks and stripes can work well. Bear in mind clothes that you already own: for example, if you possess a grey skirt and black trousers, a pattern that incorporates these two colours and one other will work very well. With the addition of a couple of blouses and a sweater, the jacket can now be worn in six outfit combinations. When buying a jacket in a striped or checked fabric, though, be careful that the patterns on different sections of the garment line up. Sleeve and shoulder, for instance, should be assembled with the pattern matching. The same applies to pockets and lapels.

For maximum flattery, the eye should always be drawn *upwards*, to the top half of your body. The fabric of the jacket should therefore be rougher and more substantial than the material of your bottom half. If you put a linen or silk jacket with a wool skirt, the weight of the lower fabric will draw the eye downwards, creating an unflattering imbalance. Always remember to consider the fabric density of your skirts and trousers before buying a jacket.

The lining should be functional and not an obvious feature of the jacket. The lining fabric should be fine rather than bulky, and in a good quality fabric that wears well. Natural fibres are preferable to man-made in this case. The colour of the lining should go with the colour of the jacket cloth. An unlined jacket

TOP LEFT

A double-breasted jacket looks best on smaller busted women. Worn with a high-necked blouse it can give a severe look, but this effect can be softened with a sweater or lower-necked blouse. Choose a longer-length jacket to disguise full hips.

TOP RIGHT

A single-breasted jacket has a slimming effect, worn long or short depending on body shape and current fashion. A simple neckline gives an uncluttered effect.

BOTTOM LEFT

A more formal style of jacket which is ideal for day into evening wear.

BOTTOM RIGHT

A shawl collar gives a softer, very feminine appearance.

will lose shape very quickly and bag at the elbows and crease and wrinkle in the sleeves. Summer jackets are often unlined; sometimes they are half-lined at the back and sleeves, and because of this will remain in better shape.

Choose colours with longevity in mind. Predominantly muted colours – navy, grey, brown and beige – are best. You might think you look terrific in bright red, but you are buying your jacket for maximum exposure. Bright red can, as I've mentioned, suggest aggression, sexiness and danger – do you want to make these suggestions to people every day? A block of bright colour can also be a strain on the eye. However, there is no reason why a jacket made in cloth with a navy background cannot have a fine red stripe in it. You can then indulge your passion for the colour by choosing a bright red blouse that picks up the colour from the jacket. Save strong fashion colours for garments that you will not necessarily be wearing in three years' time – unlike your wisely chosen jacket. The colours in your jacket are to provide the basic colours in your capsule wardrobe.

The Skirt

There is an enormous variety to choose from in skirt shapes and styles. The A-line skirt, for instance, is still very popular, although it is a shape that flatters very few women, pulling the eye downwards to focus on the lower half of the body. A-lines can also look old-fashioned and matronly. Full or very flared skirts can be impractical – you risk getting folds of material caught in a lift door, or a sudden gust of wind can send your skirt billowing upwards. A more subtly flared skirt can look good worn with a long narrow jacket which reduces its movement potential. Boots worn under it will continue the wider silhouette to the ground.

To look streamlined, a straight skirt is the best bet for most women. A straight skirt should never be so narrow that it inhibits movement, and those with a kick-pleat at the back, or a side split, are very wearable (the splits must be discreet, though). The traditional classic skirt is straight, not too narrow, often with an inverted pleat at the front. A modern version of this is narrower, with a long slit at the back, possibly surrounded by buttons. A cool wool or light-weight gabardine skirt will take you through much of the year.

When buying a shorter straighter skirt – or when having one of your old ones shortened – it is advisable to ask the alterations person to judge whether the skirt will need tapering slightly after it is shortened. This is not advice that a salesperson will generally offer or think about, but it can make a lot of difference to the look of the garment.

Pleated skirts, which seem to enjoy a recurring popularity,

TOP LEFT
'A' line skirts look matronly.

TOP RIGHT
Pleats look fattening as they 'hang' from full hips.

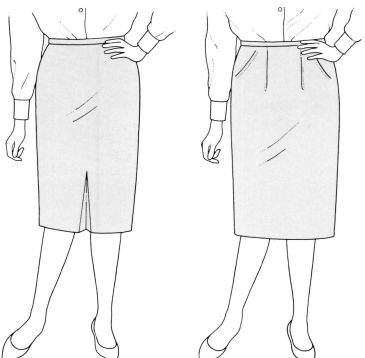

BOTTOM LEFT
A traditional classic streamline style, slightly tapered, with inverted pleat.

BOTTOM RIGHT
Soft pleats at the waist are flattering for larger sizes – pockets pointing upwards towards the centre give a slimming effect.

should be chosen with great care, as they can make you look bulky if you are not reed slim. Short pleated skirts look schoolgirlish, and pleated skirts that stop just below the knee can look matronly. On a large size, pleats work best falling flatly from a basque, as fewer and flatter pleats falling from a line lower on the torso will draw the eye away from the waist and hips. In a fully pleated skirt, with pleats starting from the waist, you add bulk to these areas. Which is why, despite the vertical lines of a pleated skirt – thought to have a slimming effect – pleats can actually be rather fattening. Pleated garments in man-made fabrics hold pleats better than natural fibres but, as the former are cheaper, they will often have a 'sheen' on them, that will not look or feel good to wear.

Another consideration concerning type of cloth is the amount you sit and how often you move back and forth on your chair. If your office is a 'workstation', for instance, and you're swivelling around from typewriter to computer and back again, then a fabric with a looser weave – some linens, for example – will wear out very quickly. Choose instead a skirt made in closely woven cloth: a wool gabardine is an excellent choice (and doesn't crease), as is a worsted, which is especially useful for those who drive a lot as well. There are very many different weights of the latter material to suit all climates.

Summer or winter, skirts should be lined: they are more comfortable to wear that way, they hang better, and crease less. Silk lining, if you can afford it, discourages static. If you buy an unlined skirt and plan to buy a petticoat to go under it, you are extremely unlikely to find one that fits well with the skirt. (Petticoats tend to be cut in a fairly 'non-specific' way, so that they can fit under a multitude of skirts. This means that they rarely 'lie' well under a skirt.) Save time and money, and ask the shop to line the skirt for you. Again natural fabrics make for the greatest comfort.

When you buy your skirt, it is most important that it fits over the hips. The waist can be altered to fit, but if the skirt is ill-fitting over the hips, it will never lie well. Bear in mind, too, if you have large hips or an ample bottom, that any extraneous detail like pockets and seaming will draw attention to the area.

Nowadays, skirts come in various lengths and no particular length has to be worn. There was a theory that skirt lengths reflected the prosperity of the nation (the prosperous Sixties were reflected in the mini, then skirt hems dropped in the Seventies' recession), but this seems to be losing ground. However, extremes in length are best avoided in business dressing. If you wear a skirt that is too short into a business meeting, you risk being appreciated for your legs rather than for what you have to say! A skirt that is too long, by reducing the proportion of your legs, will make you look dwarfed and reduce your mobility.

TOP LEFT
BACK DETAIL *adds interest to a straight skirt and looks good on all sizes.*

BOTTOM RIGHT
POCKET DETAIL *running from the side seam to the waistband draws the eye in towards the centre and helps to give a slimming effect.*

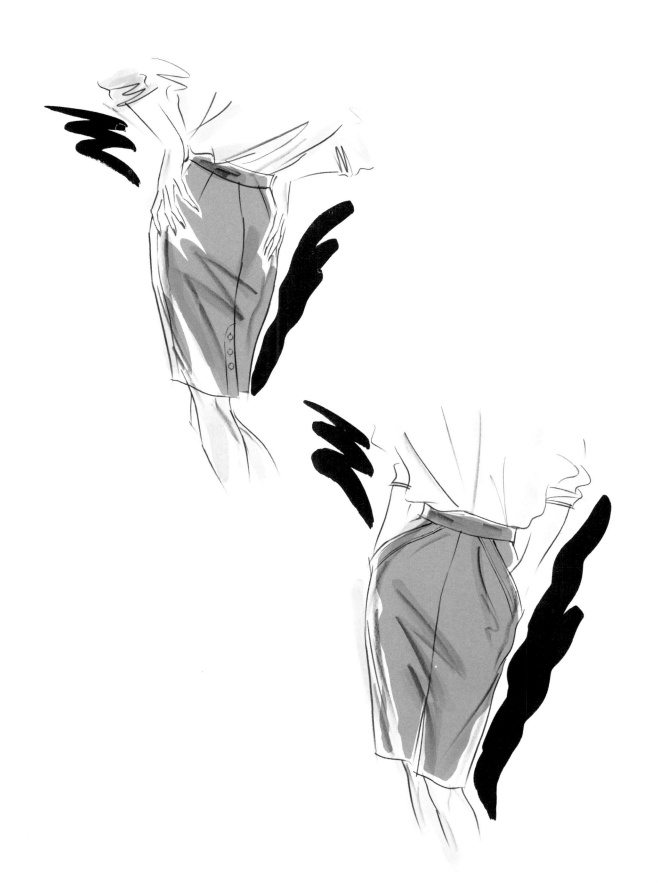

In the capsule wardrobe, the colour of your skirt should be compatible with that of the jacket. A large block of bright colour will only draw attention to your backside and lower half. A muted colour, either the same as the jacket or picking out a colour from the jacket, will look far more attractive. If you choose a skirt in the same colour as your jacket buy it in a textured fabric if the jacket is a smooth fabric, or vice versa. This eliminates the problem of dyes of the same colour varying from manufacturer to manufacturer.

THE SUIT

Everything that has been mentioned in the previous two sections applies to the suit. For someone starting out on a career, or who wants to dramatically improve her image, I believe a suit is her best investment. One particular customer was going back to work after a traumatic divorce and a number of years at home. She was nervous and uncertain how to present herself. She was stunned to see herself in one of our suits, but paled at the price tag. 'I'll buy it when I get the job,' she said, to which I replied, 'But you won't get the job if you're not dressed credibly.' I suggested she approached her bank manager for a loan. She was surprised when he was amenable, and I was not surprised when she got the job! If you really need the job, you've got to *believe* you're going to get it, so making the initial investment in the suit that will give you that necessary confidence is not unreasonable strategy . . .

If you do not think that you have a well developed enough 'eye' yet regarding cut, cloth and colour, then you are better advised to choose a suit, rather than buying a jacket and skirt separately. A well designed suit eliminates some of the decisions that you need to make. You might buy a single-breasted jacket, and then choose a skirt with a seam and split towards the side. The vertical line created by the jacket edge in the middle of the body will not look particularly compatible with the vertical line on the skirt, at the side of the body, and you will find it impossible to look streamlined. In a good suit, however, the designer will already have made these decisions for you, and the skirt and jacket will be balanced in proportion, shape and line.

There are many suits on the market today which look like air-hostess uniforms. They tend to have boxy jackets, A-line or straight skirts and to be mass-produced. These suits are dull, predictable and diminish individuality, and are worn by women who, having been given some responsibility, know they need to reflect this in their dress. These suits are an easy option, that require little thought; they are if you like, 'management-clone' dressing. Women buy them to play safe, and because they feel guilty at the thought of spending a little more money on some-

OPPOSITE PAGE
A collarless longer length jacket will give a slimmer line. The drop-necked shirt with revers adds interest to the simple neckline and a chunky necklace complements the clean lines.

thing rather more stylish. You are unlikely to get a good fit in a suit like this, and you'll probably never feel really happy in it. Far better to spend a little more on a special suit that makes you feel very confident every time you wear it.

Because the suit is a large item, the choice of cloth is very important. Stripes and checks, because the patterns are made up of straight lines suggesting order and structure to the eye, are probably the most appropriate for business. You are less likely to get tired of a subtle pattern – because it can be worn with various blouses that pick out various colours – than a plain block of colour. Even so, the main colour in a patterned suit needs careful consideration – it should go with jackets, skirts, blouses and sweaters that are already in your wardrobe.

A suit should always be lined, unless it is very light-weight for the height of summer. Light-weight fabrics like linen in deep colours – navy or brown, say – look very chic in the summer, especially when the great majority of women are favouring washed-out pastels!

Although one suit will do for the capsule wardrobe, a fully comprehensive business wardrobe might have *four* suits in it – a light-weight linen or cotton one for summer, two made in cool wool or gabardine, and a heavy wool or tweed one for the winter months. It is often a good idea to match a trouser to your skirt suit at the time of purchase, so that the suit jacket can be used for two outfits. Often trousers are available in the identical fabric.

THE BLOUSE

In terms of dressing for business, your blouse is the equivalent of the man's tie. It is the garment which can bring colour and life to an outfit, and one that you will change frequently. You will probably change your blouse every day, so you are likely to own several different ones. For a start, you should allow yourself a minimum of two.

A blouse should fit comfortably. There should be plenty of room in the armholes and sleeves for movement, and ample material over the bust. You don't want to take off your jacket to reveal perspiration stains under the arms.

Try and look for alternatives to the blouse that looks just like a man's shirt, as this can look severe and prim, especially when buttoned all the way up to the collar. An unusual collar can add a distinctive touch. Round necks, double collars and draped crossover necklines can all add interest.

You need to take into consideration the collar of the jacket that you are wearing over the blouse. Mandarin or edge-to-edge (round necks and completely çollarless) jackets will look best with a roll neck or polo neck blouse under them, or a plain scoop neckline that falls below the level of the jacket collar.

'The important thing about a suit, and I wear them a lot, is that when you take your jacket off, it should look just as smart. I want clothes that are elegant and professional and, of course, feminine ... that's important.'
Suzanna Hammond,
Managing Director,
PR company

OPPOSITE PAGE
A raglan sleeved jacket, worn with a modern version of the high-necked shirt and classic trousers, makes for a comfortable yet chic look, not too formal.

These styles of jacket should not be worn with shirt-style collars as they will look very cluttered indeed.

Rever jackets look good with shirt-type collars or lower rounded necklines, but they can look fussy with a blouse that also has revers. If you are concerned about looking over-severe in a plain blouse, then go for soft roll or shawl collars, simply and softly elegant. But try to avoid blouses with bows at the neck (a look that, up until recently, was much favoured by Britain's leading female Conservative politician), as they tend to look ageing and 'mumsy' in my opinion.

Have a look at the drawings on page 59 which show the different effects that can be achieved by wearing different shapes of blouses and T-shirts under a variety of jacket shapes.

Blouses with gently padded shoulders are often fashionable. The only drawback with this style is that if you put an already padded shouldered jacket over your padded shouldered blouse, then you can end up with enormous shoulders. Give yourself the option 'to pad' and attach shoulder pads with Velcro or lingerie clips under your bra straps.

In the summer choose blouses in cotton and linen which wash well. If you buy a blouse in silk, check that it is not transparent, and that it is not puckered by stitching at the collar and cuffs. A textured silk will not need cleaning so often. Silk shirts can be taken into work if you are going out in the evening as they can transform your suit or skirt and jacket into a far 'dressier' outfit. Avoid man-made fabrics that are very shiny for day wear, as they convey a rather glamorous impression with inappropriate connotations (would Joan Collins do well in your company?) In winter, blouses in Viyella or a mixture of wool and silk or wool and cotton are cosy.

Small dots and stripes in blouses can be combined most effectively with other patterns in your suit or jacket. Checks, which tend to remind us of farmers or lumberjacks, are rather sporty for business. Paisley or floral prints have an 'old-fashioned' look about them, and they can make you look older. A plain blouse can always be livened up with interesting jewellery.

Every season, there are strong influences on colour. Many shops only stock a very limited range of shades. If you are dying to buy something in a strong fashion colour, then a blouse, bearing in mind its limited lifespan, is your wisest choice. Buttons and button thread should all be in the appropriate colour.

A crisp, immaculately pressed blouse can create an excellent impression. It makes the strongest statement about the difference between casual and business clothing, because it looks 'labour intensive' in terms of the time required to iron it. Other people are likely to surmise that a woman who spends so much care on one item, will lavish this quality on her work.

'In designing dresses and coats, I thought first of all of execution, above all the cut, as when I made a theatre decor, I thought first of the plan. I have always thought that a dress should be built almost like an architectural work, the conception can be either based on a length of material which, cut in a variety of ways becomes the form of the dress, or based on an amusing detail, around which the dress is designed.'

Erte,
Theatrical Designer

THE SWEATER

The traditional classic sweater has a round neck and fully fashioned set-in sleeves. Its modern counterpart, like all 'modern classics' is larger fitting, with a lower collar or cowl neck and moulded shoulders. Body shapes are either much narrower or more casual today.

Casual sweaters are very useful, as you can put them with trousers or skirts, and you can easily accessorize them if you are going out for an informal evening after work. Always make sure, however, that the armholes of the sweater fit comfortably under your jacket. In winter, when warmth is a priority, it is wiser to wear a light thermal vest under a fine wool sweater rather than trying to squeeze a bulky Shetland or Aran sweater under your suit. This makes practical sense too, because layers of clothing trap air, and this keeps you warm. Dolman sleeves have larger and therefore bulkier armholes, again unsuitable under jackets.

Sweaters in wool, cashmere or a wool and silk mixture are best, rather than man-made fibres which do not feel so comfortable. Cotton sweaters or cotton mixtures are useful in the summer and, the climate in the western hemisphere being as unpredictable as it is, you can even wear light-weight wool sweaters in summer and not feel too uncomfortable. If you have a problem wearing wool next to the skin, then opt for the best quality synthetic that you can.

Classic round-necked, crew-necked or V-necked sweaters can look dull or severe. If you are wearing a sweater for business under a suit, then you don't want it to look too casual when you take your jacket off. So look around for a sweater with a shirt-style collar or a soft cowl neck, thus adding styling and formality. However, a beautifully cut T-shirt shape in a good fabric looks great under a suit both in summer and winter, and is easily available.

You should expect a sweater in a good yarn to last you for several years. It should wash well, preferably by hand. It should look good with trousers and come in useful at weekends. A loud, bright colour in this instance is not a good idea, if you intend to keep it for a while.

THE DRESS

The range of dresses available in any one season is especially susceptible to the vagaries of the fashion industry, and it can sometimes be extremely difficult to find one which is stylish and well-cut. A flouncy or frilly dress is never appropriate business dress, as it looks frivolous and you risk reminding your colleagues of their mothers or daughters, instead of conveying the impression of a professional equal.

Front-buttoning shirt dresses or coat-dresses can ring the changes with your suit in the capsule working wardrobe, as a blouse, fine sweater or T-shirt can be worn underneath. The shoulder line should always be as wide as or wider than the hips, allowing a generous amount of material to cling rather than stretch over the hips. If you are 'hippy' avoid belting the dress, as this will only accentuate the difference in size between your waist and hips. Belts should cut across the body at points you wish to accentuate, rather than features you would prefer to distract attention from. Any sort of belt also breaks up a streamlined silhouette, which is why straight coat-dresses flatter larger women.

Necklines on dresses need consideration. A high-necked dress, providing the onlooker with a large expanse of fabric for the eye, can look severe. Create relief and distraction by accessorizing the dress with jewellery. Avoid collars that have to be worn in a certain way, or a belted dress that looks fine when you are sitting down, but because of a lack of belt loops, rearranges itself when you rise. You want to be concentrating on business, not constantly titivating with your appearance. (You can always ask a shop to make loops for your garment. It's an easy job.)

Dress cloth needs to be fluid, because a dress is made up of relatively large pieces of cloth that need to move with the body. Thick, bulky materials are unlikely to lie well, and are impractical if you work in centrally heated offices. Jersey, wool and cotton gabardines and cool wools move easily and do not hold creases.

Floral prints can look demure and feminine, whilst larger floral prints on these larger areas can look overpowering. Checks and stripes can be effective but remember that you are covering most of your body in the cloth and bold patterns will be obtrusive. A straight dress with a simple cut will look better in a larger check or stripe, than a dress with an intricate cut and lots of detail.

The dress should fit in with the rest of your wardrobe, and the same colour considerations apply to the dress as to the suit. However, if you do want to buy something bright, you are better off buying a bright dress than a suit. A dress will be cheaper, and in meetings you can wear your jacket over it, which will tone down the effect. The colour should, of course, be chosen to tone with your basic jacket.

The traditional classic dress is a shirtdress with fitted-in armholes. The 'modern classic' version of this has bigger, more shapely armholes and softly padded·shoulders.

Conventionally, the dress has been worn for social events, and when women are at their most decorative. We are now seeing something of a revival in wearing dresses for business, so they should be chosen with great care.

OPPOSITE PAGE
This classic button-through dress is beautifully cut and fits perfectly. It is teamed with a toning checked jacket which could form the basis of another outfit. This will be a flexible combination – very useful for a travel wardrobe.

THE TROUSERS

A surge in the emancipation of women usually means that trousers become more popular wear – as, for example, in the Twenties and the Sixties. Conservative companies, however, still regard trousers as inappropriate dress for women in business, although many of us find them very practical. I suggest if you have any doubt over their suitability, then err on the cautious side. Certainly at interviews, presentations and meetings – when dealing with people who are an unknown quantity – you are better off in a skirt. You run no risk of being regarded as 'mannish' or 'too informal'.

Most importantly, trousers must be well-cut. They should fit snugly, not too tightly, over the hips and bottom, and not cut into you when you are sitting down. Trousers which are pleated from the waist, with straight legs – the traditionally classic line – are flattering to more curvaceous figures. The modern classic, with narrower legs that taper, look best on women with slim legs. Turn-ups help a medium- to wide-legged style hang better, weighing the cloth down slightly. Narrow trousers with turn-ups can look 'bottom-heavy'.

If you choose trousers made in a natural, closely-woven cloth, you will avoid too much creasing and bagging at the knees and bottom. Suiting material, in gabardine or lightweight wool, works well. Heavier trousers, made in tweed and denser wools, will keep their shape better and feel far more comfortable if they are lined. Nothing is more uncomfortable than itchy trousers! Linen trousers are cool and comfortable in the summer, as long as you are not worried about looking 'creased'.

For those of you who are fortunate to work in an environment where trousers are perfectly acceptable, then you might want to buy a skirted suit that has matching trousers. A trouser suit is very useful, providing that you buy it in an interesting cloth which does not date rather than in an unusual, extreme cut which *does* date.

Trousers are made up from relatively narrow pieces of cloth, and they cover a large area of the body, so large patterns and bright colours will draw the eye to the trousers, rather than the person inside them.

THE OVERCOAT

A coat is likely to be an investment, a 'major purchase' that you will use for several years. It needs to be roomy enough to comfortably wear a suit underneath, yet not so large that it looks ridiculous if you slip it over a dress for evening wear. Always try a coat on bearing in mind the range of garments it will be covering. A roomy coat can be made to look smaller by adding extra shoulder pads if it is too wide across the

'I pioneered the wearing of trousers in meetings; I didn't like the idea of a woman sitting in a meeting, whilst the men were there, thinking of patting her on the knee!'

Glenys Roberts,
Writer and Newspaper Columnist

LEFT
A classic roomy coat, useful for wearing over a suit.

RIGHT
The large coat can be made narrower by putting the revers up and adding a long scarf.

shoulders, or by lifting the revers up and tying a scarf around the shoulders. The scarf will bunch the cloth together, and draw the eye in towards the centre of the coat.

Square, lightly padded shoulders will balance out the hips. Raglan sleeves can often make women look round-shouldered, in my opinion. The classic Parisian coat – square-shouldered, double-breasted, low-buttoned with medium revers and slit, slanted or patched pocket – is very popular. A more modern version has lower revers, a long slit at the back and wider shoulders, the fit is generally 'bigger'. If the fit of one of these coats is good – ample but not drowning – you could expect to wear it for at least five years.

The coat cloth needs to be warm enough, but not too heavy. Because so many people drive to work, the old-fashioned 'heavy coat' is no longer so useful. A tweed coat, for instance, can be very heavy if you are carrying it around with you all day. Wool or, if you can afford it, wool and cashmere are good buys. I've been selling a wool and cashmere coat for many years now: it costs £380 at the time of writing and the design has remained virtually unchanged for eight of those years.

Three-quarter coats can be useful if you drive a great deal or have to keep hopping in and out of cars. A drawback, though, is that if your skirts are shortish, then in winter your legs are likely to get cold. All your bottom 'halves' need to go with the colour of the three-quarter jacket, too. I think a padded leather jacket in a three-quarter length can be a very useful buy – it's warm, light and, if belted, prevents the wind blowing up through your skirt!

Your coat colour should be chosen with longevity in mind. For this reason it is best to avoid fashion's whims and choose a neutral colour that you can live with for several years.

THE RAINCOAT

The climate in northern Europe unfortunately provides us with plenty of opportunity to wear a raincoat. But aside from its practical purpose – and with thanks to Lauren Bacall – a raincoat can ooze glamour, and provide an effective cover for evening wear.

A raincoat should be generously cut, so that you can comfortably wear your heaviest suit under it. Raincoats are very useful travelling companions, so don't buy one that is too heavy. Many are made with belts, but the belts do not always need to be worn to make the coat look good. Remember that if you choose a raincoat that *needs* to be worn belted, you could be wearing several layers under it, and that pulling in at the waist could make you look bulky.

A raincoat should protect you from the wind, as much as from the rain. Lots of flaps, deep slits and openings in the design will not do this very efficiently. Choose a raincoat that is more smoothly constructed.

The traditional classic raincoat is a Burberry. Thomas Burberry developed his secret formula for rain-resistant gabardine in the second half of the nineteenth century, and the garments that bear his name have remained relatively unchanged for decades. The modern classic raincoat is a big trench mac, with large shoulders and pockets, most usually made in stone or putty colours.

A good raincoat should last you about four or five years. If you buy one with a detachable lining then you can wear it all year round. Only very traditional raincoats have these type of linings. You can find more stylish versions, which are made with a layer of thermal lining in between the garment cloth and the lining material, giving a slightly quilted effect, and they too can afford you year-round protection from the elements.

EVENING WEAR

The amount and sort of evening wear you need will depend very much on your lifestyle. If your socializing is work-related you could still need to look businesslike in a 'dressed-up' suit; if

OPPOSITE PAGE
A big trenchcoat is very useful as it can be worn over a suit, yet will look glamorous when belted at the waist over something less bulky, such as a dress. If the collar is raised, the shoulder line will appear narrower.

you go to many formal functions then it will be worth investing in a long evening dress.

The most useful outfit for someone who only goes to 'black-tie' functions occasionally is a smart cocktail suit. A dark straight gaberdine skirt, with a soft and feminine style jacket, satin or silk blouse and large earrings, looks very smart. If you are in any doubt as to how 'dressy' you need to look, then take extra jewellery along with you in a bag. A leather suit looks particularly good after six in the evening; you can wear it all day at work, and then dress it up with a silk or satin top, and jewellery.

It can be very tempting when there is a wonderful selection of evening dresses in the shops, to buy evening wear for the social life you *imagine* you have, rather than for reality. (Most of us have an evening dress or party frock in our wardrobes that we very rarely wear.) The best stand-by is an understated evening dress, with a lowish neckline, that you can dress up or down with different necklaces. The 'little black dress' is useful too, but does not need to be taken literally: there is something very sombre about a sea of little black dresses that detracts from individuality, so your dress could be navy, brown, burgundy or any darkish colour.

If you choose trousers, add evening sweaters with a touch of glitter, or jackets in a shiny or glittery fabric. Take care that the material does not look 'cheap', or you can easily look as though you are in a circus or stage costume. Neither will cheaper fabrics 'lie' well or be comfortable to wear. Cheap thick velvet, for example, will have bulky seams and won't move with the body. In summer, a very fine pleated silk skirt, creating an illusion of slimness not bulk (because of the sheer texture of the cloth), can look very pretty, with a great variety of blouses or silky sweaters.

SOME SAMPLE 'CAPSULES'

These 'capsules' are based on an existing and loved item within your wardrobe, or on a major new purchase.

When you are starting to build a capsule wardrobe, it is a good idea to follow guidelines in order to help you develop an eye for what works and what does not. The safest colours to start off with are camel, beige or stone; black; grey; navy. Keep the basics of your capsule hanging together in your wardrobe so that you can see how the 'picture' is being built up. Keep the blouse under the suit, for instance. Very soon, you'll carry these images in your head and think about them when you want to add to your wardrobe. This way, you will be far less likely to make expensive mistakes when buying. On page 77 are some basic sample capsule ideas.

'I deal with men only and I have to strike the balance between being too frilly and too dowdy.'

Anke Harris
Managing Director,
Maplin Engineering

GREY SUIT WITH VERY FINE AQUA AND NAVY STRIPES

PLAIN NAVY SKIRT OR TROUSERS
AQUA SHIRT AND WHITE T-SHIRT
AQUA SWEATER
NAVY DRESS, PERHAPS WITH A BOLD PATTERNED SCARF IN TONES OF GREY AND AQUA
NAVY OVERCOAT OR PALE GREY RAINCOAT

For the evening, find an aqua or cream satin T-shirt – and wear pearl earrings and a ring to connect the colours. Accessorize with navy: navy bag and shoes – but go for dark slate-grey or barely black tights or stockings (the 'navy' dyes in tights always appear too blue). Wear neutral tights in the evening if your legs are good enough.

BLACK AND WHITE PRINCE OF WALES CHECK JACKET

BLACK SKIRT
BLACK AND WHITE SPOTTED BLOUSE
WHITE SWEATER, POSSIBLY WITH A BLACK TRIM
RED DRESS, WHICH COULD HAVE A BLACK COLLAR OR BLACK BUTTONS AS TRIM
BLACK TROUSERS
TAN OVERCOAT

This sort of jacket is probably the most versatile you could ever find, and it usually appears in both summer and winter collections in both winter and summer weight fabrics. Add a pair of white jeans, some sneakers and a grey and white striped cotton shirt for a casual weekend look. Accessorize with black shoes and barely black tights or stockings. Wear silver jewellery. Put a red handkerchief in the breast pocket of the jacket when wearing with the red dress, and a white handkerchief when the jacket is worn with the black and white spotted blouse and black skirt or trousers (or, more 'now', a black flower on the lapel).

DUSTY PINK JACKET

This is flying in the face of all I've been saying about neutrals and basics – but we're *all* tempted occasionally!

SOFT GREY SKIRT

DUSTY PINK/WHITE/GREY STRIPED SHIRT

IVORY SWEATER

TAUPE OR MUSHROOM DRESS

CHARCOAL GREY TROUSERS

DARK BROWN OR BLACK OVERCOAT OR RAINCOAT

Make sure that lipstick and nail polish colours are in the same shade as the jacket. Match accessories to the coat.

PLAIN STONE OR CAMEL SUIT

BLACK SKIRT

BLACK TROUSERS

BLACK, CREAM AND POSSIBLY ONE OTHER COLOUR STRIPE SHIRT

PLAIN BLACK SWEATER

BLACK OR NAVY DRESS

BLACK COAT

CAMEL RAINCOAT

Accessorize with black for black outfits, and navy if wearing the navy dress. Co-ordinate tights with shoes.
A camel suit is more difficult to accessorize for evening, but it can be dressed with loads of gold and a scarf (with a bright colour, such as emerald, red or white).

BROWN CHECK JACKET WITH CREAM, GREEN AND TAN IN CHECK

TAN SKIRT, EITHER PLAIN OR THE SELF STRIPE, OR BROWN FOR A MORE CLASSIC LOOK

GREEN AND WHITE STRIPED SHIRT

TAN BLOUSE

CREAM SWEATER

OFF-WHITE WOOL DRESS

BROWN TROUSERS, WHICH COULD HAVE A SLIGHT TAN OR GREEN FLECK

TAN OVERCOAT

Choose dark brown shoes and bags. Try to find bitter chocolate brown tights – many brown tights are too red, and look cheap.

OPPOSITE PAGE
For day, this versatile blazer jacket can be dressed up and worn over a belted sweater with sporty jewellery. For evening, the jacket can be dressed up by belting it at the waist and wearing it over a silk T-shirt with a matching or toning silk handkerchief in the breast pocket. The hair is worn up in a more glamorous style with dramatic earrings. Higher heeled shoes and darker tights make for a sophisticated evening look.

CHAPTER SEVEN

PUTTING IT INTO PRACTICE

The aim of the Wardrobe consultancy is to make a client look and feel supremely confident. So, before beginning a makeover on a client, it is important to find out about her personality and lifestyle. Although her new appearance might be quite different after the makeover, she must still retain her essential character, and mustn't feel awkward or inappropriately dressed. A truly flamboyant character will need clothes that reflect her outgoing personality, whereas an introvert will feel happier in clothes that are quieter and more controlled.

We used volunteers rather than professional models for this section, normal women, some of whom we had only met the day before. We had to be very certain that we were making the right decisions about their hair, make-up and clothes. Each volunteer felt that time restrictions for shopping and general lack of interest in clothes and fashion prevented them from looking their best. Generally, they felt that although they had a serious attitude to their careers, they lacked confidence in the image they projected, and felt in need of professional help.

In this section we do not aim to show magical transformations that are not credible or easily attainable – the reader would soon realize that such an image could never last after the photo session. The changes we have made are significant, but not dramatic. During the makeovers, we used the advice of a top make-up artist and a top hairdresser who both understand the need for a natural, easy routine for the busy woman. April works for Stephen Glass in his make-up salon, Face Facts, in central London. Face Facts advises women on skincare and make-up. Anthony, who works for John Frieda, has done work for most of the major women's magazines. He is highly regarded for his ability to take into account face shape and lifestyle in choosing an appropriate easy-care style for his clients.

PHOTOGRAPHS: SVEN ARNSTEIN

HAIR: ANTHONY YACOMINE AND SUSAN FOWLER FOR JOHN FRIEDA

MAKE-UP: APRIL FOR STEPHEN GLASS AT FACE FACTS

ALEX

Alex is a graduate of 22, who is looking for her first job in marketing. She is tall (5′ 8″) and slim (size 10), with mid-brown hair. At present, she is on a tight budget, and when she arrived was wearing what she considered to be her smartest outfit – a very plain black skirt and sweater. Although her parents had given her some money to buy a suit for interviews and work, she had been unable to find anything she liked in the high street stores.

We suggested that the best thing Alex could do to develop her image was to invest her money in a well-tailored jacket, rather than trying to buy a cheap suit. We selected a classic, long, Prince of Wales check jacket which had the effect of upgrading her basic sweater and skirt. The jacket was set off by a classic pair of fake gold and silver earrings which would combine well with any outfit.

Anthony levelled off her hair and combed her fringe back. To give the appearance of fullness and body, her hair was dried over a circular brush and styling lotion used on the roots.

As Alex has a sensitive, allergy-prone skin, April used a fragrance-free foundation. Concealer was applied under the foundation to hide her surface veins, and a translucent pink blusher and lipstick were used to brighten her rather pale complexion. To counteract her deep-set eyes, a light buff colour was dusted on the lid, and a darker navy-blue shade was used above this, which has the effect of widening the eyes.

The overall impression that Alex gives after her makeover is much more poised and polished, with a smart and businesslike air.

CATHERINE

Catherine is a 24 year-old editor with a book publishing company. She is 5′ 4″ and slender (size 8). She likes to be comfortable for work and wants to avoid the harsh 'dress for success' image. She travels abroad to book fairs, and needs to wear clothes that travel well and are comfortable, businesslike and smart enough to carry her through daytime meetings and evening receptions.

The outfit she arrived in had the effect of making her look bigger than she actually is, and was not appropriate for meetings. We put her in a leather suit which was both practical and comfortable for travelling in and could be worn without the jacket for less formal occasions. The straight skirt emphasized her slim figure, and could be worn with a blouse or sweater.

Anthony trimmed Catherine's hair and fringe and dried it straight. This helped draw attention to her wonderful bone structure, and made her look classically smart.

Catherine's fair hair and golden skin required natural make-up, in golden shades.

After the makeover, Catherine's air of international chic would have looked as smart and comfortable in Paris, Milan or Frankfurt as in London.

RUTH

Ruth is a 36-year-old music consultant who advises advertising agencies on music for commercials. She is tall (5′ 8″), and a size 12. Because of her height, Ruth looks good in most clothes, and is therefore often tempted into ill-advised impulse buys. She confessed that she had made a number of expensive mistakes because of this. She prefers wearing skirts to trousers and felt that her image needed to be successful and confident but not overpowering or intimidating.

We felt that Ruth would look her best in clothes that were stylish, shapely, and well-tailored. A beige suit was chosen for her (which also has a matching coat and trousers), and a pale green linen blouse. The outfit was complemented by a set of stylish gold jewellery – earrings, necklace, and a bracelet.

Anthony suggested that she should darken her hair a little to soften the tone – Ruth is a keen swimmer and the chlorinated swimming pool water had lightened her hair and dried it out, giving it a brassy tone. Her hair was cut an inch at the back, and slightly more at the front to frame her face, and give it fullness and width, as she has a rather long face.

Ruth has sensitive skin, which is prone to flushes – she said that it had been dehydrated by central heating and chlorinated pool water. April applied a moisturising foundation which would 'hold', and achieved a soft, golden look with apricot and taupe eye shadow, tawny cream blusher, and a deep coral lipstick. The taupe eye shadow was just dark enough to act as a foil to her deep brown eyes.

After the makeover, Ruth looked stylish and highly successful, yet very approachable, too.

TRINA

Trina is a 38-year-old illustrator's agent. She is 5′ 5″ and a size 12. She has slim hips but quite a big bust. Her job involves a lot of travelling around by car, so her main priority is to find comfortable, practical clothes. As she is in daily contact with young, creative people in the advertising world, she wants to project a youthful image, and doesn't want to look 'straight' or boring.

When she arrived, she was wearing ski pants and a big jacket, with very wide shoulders, which had the effect of shortening her neck. Her clinging blouse drew attention to her large bust, and the stretch trousers emphasized her slim hips. We thought that it was important to play down the busty look, and chose a loose fitting striped silk shirt, which looked far more subtle. As she expressed a strong preference for trousers, we suggested a classic navy pair with a matching three-quarter length coat in cool wool, which does not crease easily. The coat had big white buttons and we added bold, chunky jewellery, in keeping with her strong, positive image.

Her hair had been cut well, so Anthony simply blow-dried it away from the face to give a softer, more flattering look.

Trina's skin is clear and in good condition, with a light golden tone, and she is able to wear most shades of make-up. April combined lavender, pink, and blue eye shadow with a rich frosted pink lipstick in a similar tone, with a matching, but softer, blusher.

After the makeover, Trina still looked bright and dramatic, with an aura of fashionable sophistication.

ALIX

Alix is a 30-year-old international banking consultant. She is 5′ 6″ tall and a size 14. When we met her, Alix was dressed in an unremarkable outfit, which make her look rather middle-aged. She said that she had no confidence at all in her ability to choose clothes for herself, and usually went by her husband's advice! Alix usually plays safe, choosing plain suits for meeting clients and running courses in the City.

To try and help Alix be a little more adventurous, we dressed her in a mustard and cream button-through dress, and a single-breasted check jacket which could be worn with different skirts. Because she said her bottom was on the large side, we chose a jacket with large shoulders to redress the balance. Chunky square earrings drew the eye towards her face, and added a bolder touch.

Anthony's expertise made a dramatic difference to Alix's appearance. Her hair had been cut very square, which was unflattering to her face shape. Layering it, particularly on top, gave her hair body and movement and created a far sleeker line. Anthony suggested that stronger highlights on top would 'lift' it even further.

Alex doesn't always wear make-up, although it makes a great difference to her fine features and light colouring, adding definition. April used khaki and gold shades around her eyes, and natural beige foundation, with coral lipstick.

We thought that Alix's makeover was a dramatic transformation. She was delighted with the results, and felt confident enough in her appearance to put our suggestions into practice in future.

CINDY

Cindy is 27, and works as a head-hunter for a firm of City stockbrokers. She is tall (5′ 8″), wears size 12–14, and has large hips. Her complexion is very fair. It is important for her to appear businesslike and professional to top-level clients. Cindy described her present wardrobe as a 'disaster area'. When she arrived she was wearing a navy blue suit and a not-quite-matching navy blue jacket.

We felt that as she was fairly tall, she could carry off a more striking outfit. We chose her a green and grey suit with a rust brown stripe. Cindy was worried that her thighs looked rather heavy, so we found her a jacket that was long enough to camouflage this problem area. When choosing clothes, Cindy needs to take into account her very pale complexion, as very dark colours can look overpowering on her. The cream silk blouse flatters the delicacy of her skin colour. The outfit was brightened by the addition of a gold necklace with a hint of silver and bronze in it, and silver and gold earrings, both of which looked unusual and rather special.

Cindy's hair had been layered too much, and tended to flop down over her face, so Anthony 'scrunch dried' it using a diffuser on a hairdryer to make it look thicker.

As her skin was sensitive and porous, April applied a water-based foundation which would hold better. Cindy has very vivid blue eyes, so April suggested that she should wear claret, plum, or soft lilac eye shadow, rather than blue shades which might 'drown' her intense eye colour.

Cindy now looks distinctive and impressive – without being in any way attention seeking – ideal for the conservative City environment in which she operates.

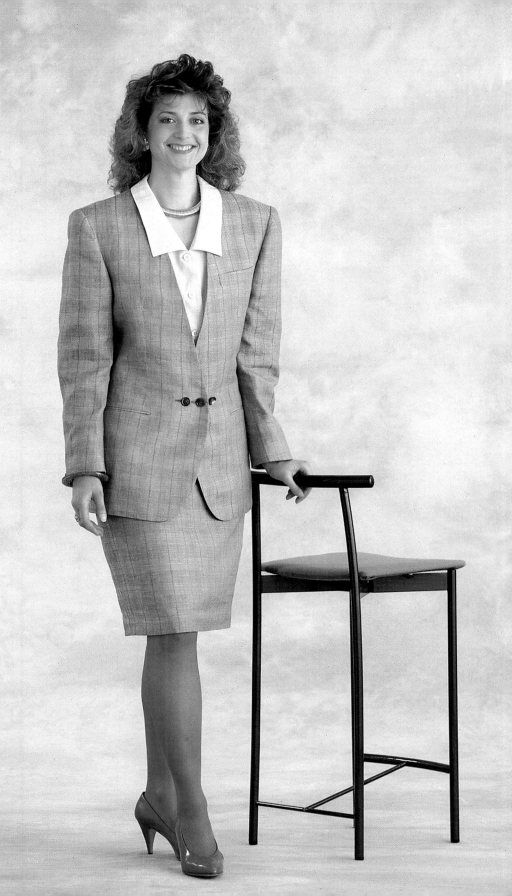

EILEEN

Eileen, the 42-year-old director of a nursing agency, is 5′ 6″ tall, and size 12. She needs to look smart for meeting clients and attending meetings, and her job demands a reassuring image without an excess of formality. Her wardrobe contains a lot of co-ordinates and some evening clothes. However, she is short of clothes that will take her from day into the evening.

Eileen's hair needed cutting, and her clothes were long and looked somewhat dated, hiding her slim figure. We felt that she should make the best of her very attractive legs, so we suggested she should try a fashionable shorter length dark brown knitted 3-piece suit. For the day, this could be worn with a cream silk blouse, gold earrings, and perhaps a long amber necklace for added colour. In the evening, she could accessorize the complete outfit with pearls and gold jewellery.

Anthony thought that her fringe needed to be less heavy, and her hair given lift and height. He trimmed her hair to an inch below the chin line, all round.

This is a versatile length that can be worn up during the day and scrunched out with lots of body for the evening.

Her sallow skin was given warmth with a rose-coloured blusher. April shaped her eyebrows, and put dusty pink and sepia eyeshadow on her lids, subtly blended. The effect was completed with a brick-red lipstick.

The finished effect flatters Eileen's svelte figure, making her look chic and businesslike, without being intimidating.

RATNA

Ratna is 39, has recently had a baby, and is about to start up a business running a hotel and wine bar. She is small, (4′ 11″), and a size 12. She needs to look smart for meeting people and promoting her business, and also needs to be comfortable, as she has to stand up for long hours, and often has to 'muck in'. She knew that the clothes she was wearing looked somewhat dated and were unflattering to her shape, but they were what she wore around the house. For work, she wanted to wear something a lot sleeker and more up-to-date.

For Ratna we chose a black linen suit with short sleeves and a 'V' neck, which is practical and extremely comfortable to wear and easy to clean. The lower edge of the jacket had a curved margin creating an inverted 'V' shape which helps to give her more height, by drawing the eye upwards. By giving her a suit jacket with slightly padded shoulders, we again focussed attention towards her face. Barely black tights and shoes, and the black suit helped to create an illusion of length.

Ratna's hair was taken up and away from the face, which helped give her more height. Anthony suggested that she should have it cut to at least shoulder length, as long hair on a small woman can look overpowering and be disproportionate.

April used a blended cream blusher with foundation on certain parts of Ratna's face where the skin tone was uneven. Deep shades of eyeshadow – shades of plum with a deep blue line on the inner rim of her eyes helped make her eyes look brighter.

After her makeover, Ratna looked as though she had shifted roles from that of new mother to up-and-coming businesswoman most successfully!

CHAPTER EIGHT

ACCESSORIES

Accessories can dramatically change the look of your clothes, and they can also be used to express your individuality. They are often made in substantial, durable materials – for instance silver, gold and leather – that should last several years. This is possibly why accessories make such a strong statement – you are expressing through them an attitude to detail, and detail that has a lifespan of several years.

Status symbols often take the form of accessories. Filofaxes, monogrammed handbags, luggage and designer sunglasses are all status symbols amongst different groups of people. Amongst the most fashionable, status symbols change very quickly and woebetide anyone sporting last season's model! The pricing of status symbols is often way above their functional value, but what they do is act as badges to show that you belong to a certain section of society – either in terms of aesthetic taste, or wealth. But the name of a designer on an object is not necessarily an indication of quality. In my opinion, the aesthetic value of a bag, for example, is considerably diminished by having the designer's name or initials emblazoned all over it. Why cover something with someone else's name, when you could have a perfectly attractive and functional plain leather bag? Status symbols are only worth having if they give you confidence, and if their status is denoted more by their quality and functional efficiency than their price.

In business, if you choose to own status symbols, then it helps if they are regarded as such by your peers. One of my friends has an excellent imitation of a Rolex watch, and she often, to her amusement, observes people noticing it and changing their attitude towards her. For if men regard their cars as status symbols, women prefer to own jewellery. Watches by Rolex, Piaget or Cartier, for instance, look good and function well besides indicating to others that you are not doing too badly for yourself. In fact, the *best* sort of status symbols are functional ones, such as watches, rather than purely decorative ones, like diamonds. You would probably buy yourself a watch, and the amount of money spent on it would be justifiable, because it is practical. Diamonds, however, are far more likely to have been bought *for* you, and could diminish your impression of self-sufficiency!

Apart from status symbols, however, the market for accessories such as shoes and boots, belts, lingerie and bags, is huge, and the discriminating shopper needs to pick her way through it with discernment. There is a definite flair to accessorizing skilfully, and to learn to do so can complete your carefully planned, professional picture.

'Shoes are a much more important accessory than many people appear to think, particularly if you call on clients a lot. In the visitor's chair, they attract a lot of attention.'

Jane Cooper,
Senior Manager, Banking

SHOES AND BOOTS

We all need to cover our feet, and most of us have far too large a collection of disparate footwear. Cut, cloth and colour – although in a slightly different sense – have relevance again here, as does my 'less is more' theory. By *thinking* first, and buying later, you can accessorize sensibly with shoes, and complement your working wardrobe perfectly as well as economically.

If you buy good quality shoes and care for them, you should only need two pairs of shoes a season. Indeed a classic court shoe, in a neutral colour with an oval toe and medium heel, should last you several years.

When you buy shoes, always walk around in them in the shop and make sure that they are wide enough. Some Italian shoes, for example, are made in narrow fittings, and if your shoes are uncomfortable, it shows on your face. Allow for the fact that in hot weather your feet can swell. Conversely, shoes that are too wide or too long will be constantly slipping off, which could make you feel and look unsure.

Unless your feet are one of your best features, avoid T-straps and ankle straps. They draw attention to the feet and make the legs look shorter by creating lines across them. Depending on fashion, court shoes will have oval, round, almond or more pointed toes. Try to choose shoes with fronts that cover the base of your toes – the cracks between toes are not the prettiest part of the anatomy.

Sling-backs look best worn with dresses, though they can be impractical in that they often slip off, and your heels can get very dirty if you are wearing them all day in the city. In my opinion, they look too casual and insubstantial to be worn with suits. If the weather is very warm, then peep-toe court shoes are a good idea.

Heel shapes vary between narrow, thick and conical. The

thickness of your shoe heel can complement the density of the fabric you are wearing: a tweed suit will look best with a thick, clumpy heel; a silk dress with a narrower one. Shorter skirts look better with higher heels because more of the leg is on display, and the higher heel elongates the leg. That is not to say that shorter skirts cannot be worn with flat heels – the look is just more sporty. Longer skirts look better with flatter heels. If you are short, avoid the mistake of buying very high heels – their relative proportion and the effect they have on your posture will only draw attention to your lack of inches. Very high heels are inappropriate for business wear anyway, as they could be uncomfortable, can look tarty, and hinder movement. I would suggest a top heel height of 2–2½ inches (5–6cm).

Always buy shoes in good leather, with real leather rather than man-made soles. Leather soles wear better and let your feet breathe. Some fine kid shoes can only be wiped over rather than polished, and will be spoilt by rain. If you are buying shoes for all weathers then buy leather which can be polished, and weather-proof the shoes before wearing them.

Suede shoes need a lot of attention to keep them looking good. Often suede is rougher looking than most leather, and will look good with denser fabrics such as tweed. You can create relief in an all-leather outfit, such as a suit, by wearing suede shoes when leather shoes would be overpowering.

Shoe shops are always full of coloured shoes at sale time, because they have such a limited lifespan. Even for special occasions like weddings, I'd advise you to choose shoes in a good neutral colour, rather than hunting high and low for shoes to go with the particular shade of your outfit. One of my favourite and most useful neutrals is tan, which goes with black, navy and grey as well as the more obvious browns and beiges. Tan shoes are not that easy to find in the shops, so if you see a good pair, snap them up. It is also a colour that can be worn all year round.

SHAPES TO SLIM THE FOOT

1 *Court shoe*
2 *Flat shoe – the bars are good for narrow feet*
3 *'T' bars are unflattering for most feet*
4 *Trouser shoe – good for short people as it gives length to the leg*
5 *Simple, low-heeled boot*

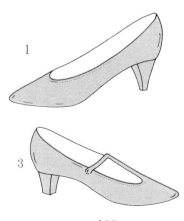
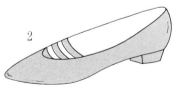

We wear boots largely for warmth and to keep our feet and legs dry. They are uncomfortable to wear all day so I would suggest you change into shoes at work. Boots rarely look flattering worn with shorter skirts, as the leg is shortened by two lines, the top of the boot and the hem of the skirt. If shorter skirts are fashionable, then at least make sure that your coat is long enough to cover the top of your boots. Small thick heels or flat heels are most practical. High heeled boots can look slightly fetishistic, and you risk misinterpretation. If you want to wear heels with trousers, the boots or shoes should have low thick heels, continuing the line of the trouser legs.

Finally, it must be said that people pass judgement on others through all sorts of signals, and many people regard the state of someone's shoes as very revealing. Scuffed, down-at-heel shoes will not make a good impression . . .

Colette in Vogue in 1925 'Every woman wants more than one bag; she wants a useful marketing and shopping bag, dainty theatre and tiny vanity bags for going out with, she would like one to match every costume.'

Colette in *Vogue*,
from *A Fashion for Extravagance,*
Sara Bowman

BAGS

The working wardrobe needs two bags in it: a large one for your day-to-day work requirements, and a smaller bag for social requirements. If you own a briefcase you may well not need the larger bag.

The classic large bag is satchel shaped, and roomy enough to carry everything you need from folders to a spare pair of shoes. It is usually a rectangular shape. I do not think that a bag necessarily needs to be in the same material as your shoes, but the colour should fit in with the predominant neutrals in your wardrobe. Some stockists, like Fendi, make high quality, man-made material bags, which compare well in quality and size with similar leather ones. These bags also come in non-specific neutral tones like taupe, which goes with every colour, and of which it would be difficult to find the leather equivalent. If you own leather and suede shoes then you could buy a bag with a leather or suede trim which would go with both.

Simple bag and briefcase shapes

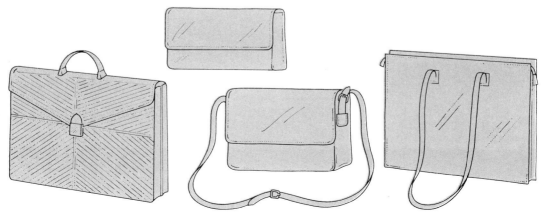

Consider your size when choosing bags, and the fit of your clothes. A large woman in a large roomy coat will look disproportionate if she is carrying a small bag, and vice versa.

Simple shapes, with stitching in the same colour as the bag work well. Check that the frame of the bag looks secure and that the leather covers the frame comfortably, and is not stretched tightly over it. The clasp should look strong and not too fiddly, and the frame and pockets in the bag should not weigh it down too much. You don't want to have to carry around a great load all day!

Shoulder bags are very practical. Ensure that the shoulder strap is wide enough for the bag and the weight you will be carrying around in it, otherwise you risk the strap cutting uncomfortably into your shoulder, or worse, snapping. A bag that has a detachable shoulder strap, and an extra strap so that you can carry it like a briefcase is especially useful if the shoulder strap is cutting into padded shoulders. You can also get larger bags that look like large elegant shoppers, and can hold a great deal of paraphernalia.

If you carry a briefcase you still might want to carry a small shoulder bag with your personal effects in it. A small clutch bag, again with detachable shoulder strap is very versatile: you can use it every day for work, and detach the strap for dressier occasions.

Your day-to-day bag is often literally the wrapper on your work, and it should reflect your attitude to its contents. All bags should be cleaned and, if leather, they should be polished regularly. Above all, avoid that travesty of elegant presentation – the plastic carrier bag.

BUT A FILOFAX IS NOTHING LIKE A PAD.

BRIEFCASES

Good briefcases for women are difficult to find, and men's briefcases tend to be heavy and cumbersome, making them look incongruous when carried by women. It is as though you are saying, 'I am not really comfortable in this role of executive woman.' A well-worn leather briefcase, that suits you, shows that you are comfortable and familiar in this part.

I like soft briefcases that are large enough to carry all your requirements. They do not need to have the heavy frames and sharp angles of men's briefcases. Make sure that they have enough pockets for you to be organized, and again that they are not too heavy.

Good briefcases are expensive, but will last you for five or six years and will probably be used every day. A strong 'case', I think, for investment buying!

If you are having difficulty finding one, then a large document case will tide you over until you find one you like.

Briefcase and Desk Accessories

Even your most functional possessions like pens, diaries, purses and key rings can say a great deal about you. Letters that are signed in ink look very distinguished, and a good fountain pen is a stylish accessory that will last you for years.

I think the enormous popularity of Filofaxes illustrates just how important it is today to appear to be organized. It instils confidence in others if you appear to have your life 'under control'.

Diaries and address books that are leather-bound, in a neutral colour like black or brown, look expensive. A tatty version of either of these suggests that neither appointments or contacts are particularly important to you. A purse should have ample room for your credit cards. Your purse is literally 'your covering on your money' and says what your attitude is towards the contents – whether you are comfortable about what you earn. If you buy lunch for clients, you will look a lot more professional paying for it out of a smart leather purse, rather then a floppy fabric pouch.

We rarely consider key-rings as accessories, and yet they are significant in that the 'means of access' to your property is attached to it. A key-ring can be viewed as a piece of jewellery.

SHE'S OUT TO LUNCH

Belts

A good belt can make a garment, so it's well worth building up a belt wardrobe. Choose them in the neutrals – black, brown, navy, grey – and you should only need to buy one of good quality per year. The buckle is the most important feature, so if you wear a lot of gold or silver then choose your metal buckle accordingly. Simple buckles, without logos, ornate designs, gilt and colour work best. Stitching is also to be considered: whether you choose a leather, skin or man-made fabric, it should be even, the right tension and without hanging loose ends. The backing on a belt is important too, and leather, suede and skin belts should always be leather backed.

If you buy a belt in the same fabric as an outfit, remember that if it is stiffened, the backing can easily come away during the dry-cleaning process. Also the buckle may fray. But, if you choose not to dry-clean the belt, then outfit and belt might just end up being slightly different colours! So, when choosing a garment with matching belt, try and visualize how a leather or suede belt would look with it too. Some self-fabric belts, for instance those in raincoats, have no stiffening and so there is no problem.

When you send a belt with a fabric buckle to the cleaners, undo the stitching and remove the buckle first. I have never come across a belt with a fabric-covered buckle where the buckle outlives the belt. When the buckle does fray, look for a metal or plastic one to replace it.

Choose the colour of your belt to go with your shoes, if you want to draw attention to your waist and look coordinated. If you don't want to over-define the waist area, than choose a belt in the same colour as the outfit. I think this is very much more chic. In my opinion, the only time that you could use a contrast colour is when you're very young with a very trim waist. The stitching should always be in the same colour as the belt.

Very thick belts can be uncomfortable. I suggest as a general rule that the denser and rougher the fabric you are wearing the thicker (not wider) the belt, the better. So with denim you could go for a chunky tan leather belt; with satin, a slim calf one. And, just a tiny piece of advice, if wearing a white blouse and black trousers or skirt, always wear a *black* belt.

Also bear in mind the size of the belt loops when wearing a belt. A narrow belt threaded through wide belt loops looks incongruous. Too-wide belt loops can always be stitched up or made narrower.

JEWELLERY

Jewellery can transform an outfit from something understated into a dressy glamorous look. It is also extremely portable, and very useful when going on to a social function after work.

There is a wide and good selection of costume jewellery on the market these days, especially in large department stores. At the time of writing, you can buy a set of costume jewellery – earrings, necklace, pin or bracelet – for about $100. Jewellery design has boomed in the past few years, and if you can afford to wear all genuine gold and silver, then you will find plenty of choice. If you can't afford this, then I suggest that you buy one good piece of jewellery, a watch or a neck chain, that you wear most of the time. With one prominent genuine gold or silver piece, the impression your costume jewellery creates will benefit by association.

Always wear jewellery that complements your size: large chunky jewels will look overpowering on a diminutive woman, whilst tiny pearls will get lost on a large woman. Jewellery should never look obtrusive with business dress, and if your clothes are stylish, too much jewellery will detract from them. Some simple shapes in gold, silver or pearl will look far more effective than weighing yourself down like a Christmas tree. Choose your jewellery to go with your clothing too: a fine navy or grey gabardine might look very 'cold' if you accessorized with silver, and can be 'warmed up' by adding gold. Pearls help black fabrics look softer as they give light to the face, especially in earrings. A chunky tweed suit will be complemented by the warmth and depth of tortoiseshell; a linen suit on the other hand could be set off beautifully by an ivory bracelet.

OPPOSITE PAGE

TOP LEFT
Earring shapes for the oval face.

TOP MIDDLE
Earring shapes for the round face.

TOP RIGHT
Earring shapes for the long face.

BELOW
Useful necklace and brooch shapes.

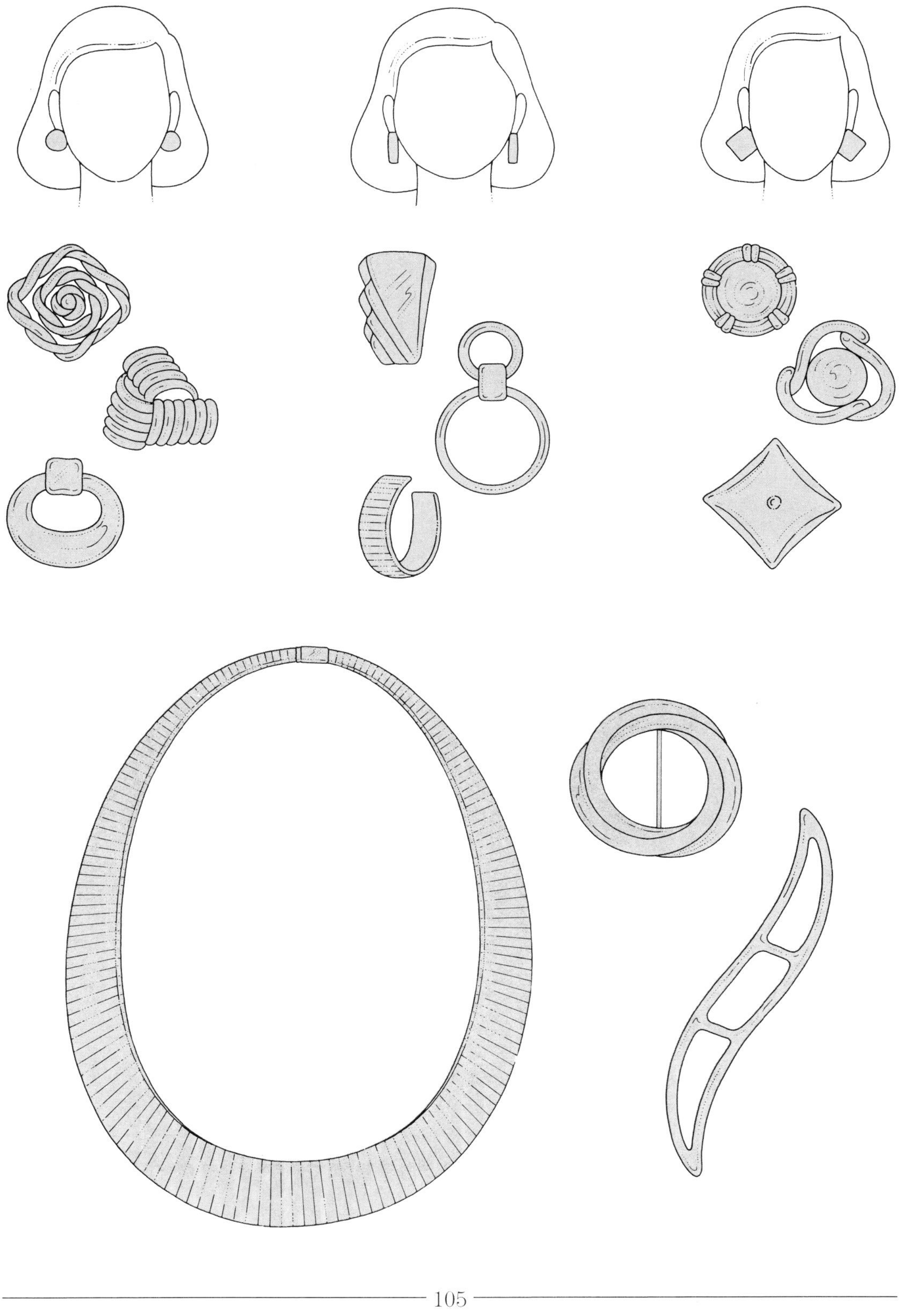

You can apply the blue/yellow guidelines to your choice of metal: if you have yellow-based colouring you might want to opt for jewellery that is predominantly made of gold; if you are blue-toned then you could choose predominantly silver.

I never feel that a woman looks properly dressed if she is not wearing earrings. On short-haired women, larger earrings soften the effect and prevent a severe look. For work, choose them in gold, silver or pearl rather than coloured plastics or sparkly stones. Dangly earrings shorten the neck and are distracting, so save them for the evening. Shapes should be simple, and enhance or repeat the patterns and lines that you are wearing. If you are sporting a striped or check suit in an angular cut, then square or triangular earrings will look terrific. If you are wearing a softly rounded knitted suit, then round or oval earrings would be more appropriate. Some women are allergic to non-precious metals, and coating the posts of earrings for pierced ears with nail varnish can help alleviate the reaction.

Short necks are accentuated by choker style necklaces, while a longer necklace will elongate the neck. However, if you have a long neck, then a necklace that rests on the collarbone will flatter you. To get the proportions right, *always* try necklaces on before buying them. Necklaces made in two metals, gold and silver, are very versatile, because they enable you to wear either gold or silver in your other pieces of jewellery. A plain ribbed necklace will reflect light up on to the face, lightening shadow. Pearls also create a very softening effect, and bring relief into dark outfits.

A plain looking jacket can be brightened up by a clip brooch on the lapel. Brooches accentuate a woman's femininity because they are an item not usually worn by men. Avoid mock rubies and emeralds which can look cheap, and opt instead for semi-precious stones, pearls, silver or gold. Brooches at the neck can make you look prim and 'buttoned up'.

Bracelets can be impractical, and irritating to yourself and other people if they jangle every time you move your arm. One simple chunky bracelet will look effective and not distract. Textured materials like tortoiseshell, ivory, ebony and wood make great bracelets, as the simple largish shapes show the texture of these materials to their best advantage.

Keep rings discreet and I would suggest that if you want to wear diamonds, then an antique ring will not look as glittery and ostentatious as a newer one. You want to look like someone that functions well, rather than an ornament.

On the subject of fashion, 'One must forgive it everything. It dies so young.'
Jean Cocteau,
Writer (1889-1963)

GLASSES

The frames of your glasses should be chosen so that they go with most of your clothes, and so that the shape suits your face.

If your face is too square or round, or your features are very angular, then do not reiterate these lines and shapes in your choice of frames. If the bridge of your glasses is high then this will accentuate a long nose.

If you've delicate colouring, strong black and white frames will look very harsh and detract from your features. Nowadays there are a large number of opticians supplying a great variety of choice in glasses frames and contact lenses, so any woman needing help with her eyesight is amply catered for.

I find that my eyes frequently get sore and tired, so I took some frames that I liked to an optician and got him to put in some lightly tinted glass, which also reacted with sunlight. I find these glasses a most useful accessory, indoors and out.

LINGERIE

Good lingerie that fits is the basis of an effective wardrobe. There is an enormous range available now, from frankly feminine lacy French knickers and camisoles to very sporty simple cotton pants and vests. Lingerie should be comfortable and make you feel good, and should enhance whatever you are wearing over it. Superb clothes can actually be ruined by wearing ill-fitting lingerie underneath.

I'd advise that you always try bras on before buying. If you are large busted, make sure that the cup size is adequate, because the cups provide most of the support. You might feel most secure in an underwired bra, though take care that the wiring is comfortable. Bra straps should be wide enough so that they do not cut into you – you do not want folds of flesh bulging out from above the cups or under the arms. Fortunately, for larger women, bras are now made to fit under every style of clothing, so that you can even get ones that do up around the waist to wear with backless dresses.

For a very smooth line, the 'body', an all-in-one undergarment, almost like a swimsuit, is very comfortable. These do up under the crotch, and it is important for the sake of comfort that they do up with large poppers, instead of buttons or hooks and eyes. 'Bodies' are perfect for wearing under knitted clothes or cotton jersey.

Pants should also fit snugly, otherwise ugly lines will show through your clothes. One of the prettiest shapes has high cut legs which dip down in the front at the waistline. Always buy pants with cotton gussets. If you feel that you need some support over your tummy, then support tights are comfortable. Wearing tights with a cotton gusset will stop 'visible pantie line' when wearing tight skirts or trousers as you don't need pants as well. If you find G-strings comfortable, they also help create a smooth line. French knickers, although very pretty, can be bulky under close-fitting clothes.

'Without foundations, there can be no fashion.'
Christian Dior,
quoted in *Dress and Undress, A History of Woman's Underwear,*
Elizabeth Ewing

Bear in mind the colour of your top layers when buying underwear, as it can show through, particularly at the height of summer. If you do not want to have to bother to think about this, then flesh-coloured lingerie is all-purpose.

Silk underwear is an extravagance, albeit a delicious one. Natural fibres will need ironing, whereas polyester does not. I suggest every woman should have the indulgence of one set of silk underwear – the sensation is wonderful next to the skin, and makes you feel very special.

If you buy lined skirts, then petticoats will be redundant in your wardrobe. If you have need for a slip, then a straight one without detail is best, worn literally as an 'underskirt', with the same fitting considerations that apply to the skirt.

Specialist underwear – sports bras, thermal underwear, vests with padded shoulders – can all be very useful. I would urge everyone to experiment with different sorts of underwear from the vast range available.

One of the most useful pieces of lingerie for the working woman is a dressing gown in a fabric that either feels very cosy, like towelling, or something more sensual, like silk. Just the thing to slip into after a hard day in the office and a long soak in the bath. A towelling robe can, of course, double up as a beach robe.

BEWARE !

DARK UNDERWEAR.

TIGHTS AND STOCKINGS

The density of your tights and stockings needs to match what you are wearing. A tweed suit needs hosiery of a thicker density than a silk dress, which will look better with very fine tights or stockings.

As a general rule, you should wear tights that are the same colour as your shoes to create the impression of a long sleek leg. However, if you are wearing coloured shoes, white or red for example, then natural coloured hosiery will look best. It is virtually impossible to match coloured shoes to coloured tights and stockings accurately, and very often coloured tights are made in lurid colours that scream at you. White tights, which became popular in the Sixties, are unflattering to all but the spindliest of legs; with navy blue shoes, dark grey tights can work well.

In winter, buy 20–40 denier tights, in summer 10–15 denier. I often wear barely-black tights even in the height of summer, but in the sheerest of deniers. I think it is inappropriate for women in business not to wear tights or stockings as it suggests a lack of formality. After all, you don't see men discarding their socks, and doing business barefoot in sandals! In very warm weather, you could wear 'hold-ups', stockings with elasticated tops that keep themselves up.

You can avoid laddering tights when you put them on by

keeping a tube of hand-cream in the drawer where you keep your tights. Every morning before you put your tights on, quickly rub a drop of hand-cream over your hands. This will prevent rough skin catching on the tights. Also, remember to keep your feet soft by using a pumice stone, and moisturizing them after a bath or shower.

Lacy or patterned tights or stockings draw attention to your legs, and are best kept for social wear. In winter, ribbed or textured tights can be very snug. Stockings and suspenders are like ' by many women (and men!), but they do show through on clingy clothes and can be uncomfortable.

Always keep a spare pair of tights in your bag or in a drawer at the office, or in the car. There is nothing worse than having to go to a meeting with a ladder in your tights.

SCARVES

The wearing of scarves tends to follow current fashion trends. In the early Seventies, for instance, it became very fashionable to wear skirts and matching shawl-type scarves around the shoulders. Indeed stole-type scarves can look elegant and serve a practical function in keeping you warm.

Cashmere or cashmere and wool mixtures made into long rectangular scarves create a soft line between your face and the collar of a coat. As well as keeping you warm, they cover a pale neck that can look very bare in winter. Choose a colour that really complements your hair or skin colouring. In recent years, yellow and red cashmere scarves have become very popular, especially amongst 'media types': it's possible that the bright streak around their necks implies a reluctance to conform. Certainly, in the depths of winter, a jewel-bright scarf can look very cheery.

Avoid cravat-type scarves and silk scarves tied around the neck – they look masculine and fussy respectively. However, in general, well designed clothes were not orginally conceived of as needing clutter, and a small scarf can look especially irritating. They have no real function, and they don't necessarily have the dramatic and aesthetic impact that a brooch or a necklace has. They can be useful, though, for dressing up a garment, but you must choose good fabrics which tie well. If you are going to wear a scarf, always wear one that has a purpose and makes a statement.

'One of the nicest things about improving one's image is the unexpected compliments you receive from complete strangers – like the girl at the University of Surrey who said to me, "What lovely tights", and the van driver in the City who called me over – for directions I thought – he said, "I like your style!".'

Jane Cooper,
Senior Manager, Banking

HATS

Hats can be either practical – keeping you warm in cold weather (for we lose a great deal of body heat through our heads) – or frothy or stylish confections to match an outfit for a special occasion. A hat will always get you noticed.

The popularity of hats depends on how formally people are dressing at a particular time, and on the current hairstyle trends. Very full hairdos, for instance, do not show hats off to their best advantage. The proportions must be right, and shorter, neater haircuts, or long hair tied up, look best with hats. Some hat styles – the beret, for instance, which does not have structured lines – can look good on long straight hair. Body proportions must be considered too when choosing a hat, of whatever type: a small woman will look dwarfed by a hat with a very large, wide brim, and a larger woman will look ungainly in a pill-box.

On a limited budget, you are best buying a hat in the base colour of your wardrobe, so that you can wear it with either a suit or a coat. Keep the lines similar: if your suit or coat has geometric revers and pockets, then an angular hat will complement these. On the other hand, if your outfit has rounded shoulders and lapels, or is soft and flowing, a hat in a rounder shape will look more appropriate. A high crown can give you extra height.

It is a good idea if you are going to a wedding to try and buy the outfit and the hat in the same shop, as they are likely to stock both items in similar shades. And always, if you are trying to buy a hat to match an outfit, take the outfit *along* with you. If you are ever having trouble matching hat to outfit, you can always dress up a natural straw hat by adding a scarf, ribbon or veiling, or silk or dried flowers in the appropriate colour from a haberdashery counter.

A basic trilby shaped felt hat, which can be worn with brim up or down is a classic. You can dress it up by adding ribbon or an accessory such as feathers or a brooch. More outrageous hats can be fun, but they are likely to have a very limited lifespan. The most outrageous designs are most effectively sported by the extrovert and confident.

Because hats are not so common these days (40 years ago women could not be smartly dressed *without* one), we often feel slightly nervous and self-conscious about wearing them. But they can look marvellous, if chosen well, and it is encouraging that hats are regaining popularity, along with the return to smarter, tailored dressing.

HANDKERCHIEFS

I have noticed a revival of real handkerchiefs rather than the usual tissues. Again it's fashion – but they are feminine and special, therefore separating you from the masses. They make an appreciated gift now, even if only used on special occasions, and I must say I do prefer using them. Silk handkerchiefs are also very useful as decoration for a jacket breast pocket especially if you choose a fabric whose design and colour coordinates

'We can't afford to be lost in the crowd – we have to stand out.'

American lawyer

with your clothes. This is an accessory that you can buy and design yourself.

Umbrellas

Umbrellas are easily lost or forgotten, but are invaluable in our unpredictable climate. I find a plain black collapsible type the most useful as I can keep it can my briefcase, and it goes with all my outfits. Dark neutral colours will make your umbrella look more expensive.

Gloves

Gloves add the final touch to a formal outfit, and in winter are essential to keep hands warm. They should match your shoes and fit comfortably across the knuckles. Most wardrobes only need one or two pairs: I would suggest leather with a wool or silk lining.

CHAPTER NINE

THE TOTAL LOOK

Buying clothes that suit you and that look good, and knowing how to accessorize them well, will not alone transform your image. Good grooming, knowing how best to wear your hair and make-up, poise and a relaxed attitude – amongst others – are just as important. At Wardrobe, we often recommend hair and make-up experts to our clients, for instance, so they can revaluate their complete look.

To look good, you have to *feel* good. In *Breaking the Glass Ceiling*, a study of top female management executives, those under scrutiny are described thus: 'Most were impeccably dressed, usually in a tailored suit but sometimes in an expensive looking dress. Some of these women were short, some a bit plump. Some were unusually tall, with a towering presence. Many appeared to be in good physical condition. Although physical health isn't often a factor considered in studies of executive stress, we believe that it should be – the energy has to be there.' Certainly, coping with stress and conserving energy are of prime importance to the working woman.

Many of you will feel quite happy with the way you are. But if you consider your image important, there is always more that you can learn from experts. Getting specialist advice on health and fitness, posture and relaxation as well as hair and make-up can save you a great deal of time and money-consuming mistakes. The expert can educate you and help you reappraise some of your established ideas about yourself.

YOUR HAIR

You can find a good hairdresser either through personal recommendation or reputation. If you are fairly bold, you can even go up to a woman whose hair you like and ask her where she has it done.

'I've even sent a few (female clients) to my hairdresser just down the street from the office. Sometimes I meet with resistance and anger. But what we're here to teach them, though, is how to succeed in the job market. The fact is that people look more at women in terms of grooming than they do men. It's not fair, but that's the way it is.'

Phyllis Dunnam,
Vice-President of Drake Beam Morin,
(Management Consultants) quoted in
The Times

A first visit to a new hairdresser always involves a certain amount of trial and error; the more familiar they are with your hair and lifestyle the better the service that they are likely to provide. So be as forthcoming about yourself as you can be, and express all your ideas about your hair. That way you minimize the risk of misunderstanding.

Sometimes, certain hairdressing salons have 'house-styles' that they foist on everyone regardless of whether the style suits the client's face or hair. Don't allow yourself to be bamboozled by a hairdresser, or let them shroud what they are doing in glamorous mystique – they are providing a service for which you are paying, in much the same way that an accountant or lawyer does!

The prime consideration for a good hairdresser when cutting your hair should be the shape of your face. You can take an admired photograph in with you, but you must allow for the fact that the model might have quite a different face shape and different texture of hair.

'One of the most important things a hairdresser should consider is the shape of your face – if you've a wide heavy jaw, for instance, the last thing you want your hairdresser to do is to cut your hair so it accentuates this feature. Your haircut must emphasize your assets'.

Anthony,
John Frieda

STYLE

Most working women want a hairstyle that is easy to keep and that can be done with a minimum of fuss in the mornings, and revived easily for the evening.

Avoid having your hair layered in the hope of creating greater volume. Haircuts with a lot of layering can easily end up looking very messy. If you have fine hair, and little time in the morning, then a short haircut that you can quickly blow dry after leaping out of the shower is easiest. If you have short hair that tends to go limp, then you could keep a portable butane gas heated roller-brush in the office, for a quick 'lift'.

Chic French and Italian women often wear their hair all one length, to the shoulders or just above. This takes about 15 minutes to dry. Curly or wavy hair can also be cut in this way, and fine straight hair can be treated with a body perm.

Shoulder length hair can be very versatile – you can put it up or back, either to look glamorous for evening wear, or when it is dirty and you want to wear it off your face. You can 'revive' this style for evening by combing it back into a pony tail, lacquering it down and adding bows or clips. (In Wardrobe, we use 'wot-nots', elasticated fabric devices that hold the hair back, yet create a far sleeker, less fussy shape than a bow.)

Long hair on an older woman is rarely flattering; by drawing the eye downwards, it makes the features look tired. There is nothing worse than a woman with a 'matured' face, who seems to be desperately holding on to her youth by sporting long girlish tresses. A younger woman, however, can make herself look more sophisticated and older by sweeping her long hair back.

In the way that you should consider your body shape and

proportion when choosing clothes, you should also take your size and the proportions of your features into account when choosing a hairstyle. A small woman, for instance, can look dwarfed by a great mass of long hair, and a close-cropped hairstyle on a broad woman can make her body look wider than it should.

Consider proportion in terms of the shape of your face, emphasizing your best features and drawing the eye away from your weaker ones. A long face will be flattered by creating width at the sides; if you have a very square jaw, or a receding chin, then disguise that area by having the hair cut so that it falls fully over the jawline. A large nose will be given greater prominence if the hair is plastered flat on the head; instead choose a style with volume on top or at the sides to balance the profile.

You also need to take your individual image into consideration when choosing a hairstyle. If you dress smartly, often in tailored clothes, then your hair will look best if it is sleek and neat. This doesn't necessarily mean a short geometric cut; you could have a gentler look with soft waves.

Because your hair frames your face, the hairstyle you choose can suggest a great deal. Some women hide behind their hair, using long fringes and full sides to hide their faces. Very short hair can look aggressive. One of the quickest ways to look more confident is to sweep hair back at the sides and create more volume on the top.

A short neat haircut will give an impression of order and control; a plethora of frothy curls will suggest frivolity. Spiky hair (now very 1970s) will suggest a rebellious nature. Careful thought should go into your choice of hairstyle; it should enhance and further your image.

COLOUR

Hair colouring is now accepted as a form of make-up, and it is a cosmetic used very successfully by many women. Your hair colour fades as you get older and lightening your hair subtly can 'lift' your features dramatically. Hair colour should always be chosen to flatter your colouring and features, however, rather than making a drastic change. A blonde who darkens her hair to a deep brunette will look pale and washed-out unless she wears a great deal of make-up. Our natural hair colour complements our skin tones, so an extreme change will involve a total re-think over the way you look and considerable maintenance in colouring roots frequently.

Covering up grey hair effectively can be a problem. A complete permanent tint can look harsh, dries the hair, and roots will need regular retouching. Streaks, high- or low-lights will need less maintenance and can be most effective for 'blending-in' the grey hairs.

COVERING UP GREY HAIR CAN BE A PROBLEM.

HAIR CARE

Your state of health is reflected in your hair, and stress and a poor lifestyle will manifest themselves in weak hair, bad condition or, at worst, handfuls of hair falling out. A good diet, exercise, fresh air, and lots of sleep are the best hair 'conditioners'.

Use a 'frequent use' shampoo if you wash your hair daily, and condition it every time you wash it. A good conditioner should not leave a residue in your hair, and will effectively act as a barrier to pollution in a city environment. If you have the time and money, then treat yourself to a deep-conditioning treatment at a salon, otherwise give yourself one at home every six weeks or so. In the summer, protect your hair from the sun with the appropriate product.

No woman feels happy with her appearance if her hair is awry. To keep hair well-maintained, I'd suggest a visit to the hairdresser once every six to eight weeks for a cut, and once every twelve weeks for high- or low-lights. Besides helping you keep up appearances, why not sit back and relax for a change!

SKIN CARE

Skin condition is a good general indicator of health, and if you smoke or drink heavily, eat poorly or have trouble sleeping, then your skin will be affected.

Before choosing skin products, you need to identify your skin type – whether it is dry, greasy, normal or combination. The best way to do this is either at a beauty salon, when you are having a treatment, or at a reputable skin-care counter in a large store. If you don't know your skin type, then you can easily end up buying products that are unsuitable.

Every woman, whatever her skin type, should cleanse, tone and moisturize in the morning and cleanse, tone and nourish in the evening. Your basic skin-care 'wardrobe' should include cleanser, toner, moisturizer and a gentle eye make-up remover that doesn't drag the delicate area around the eyes. There is an enormous range of skin-care products on the market from primers and neck creams to tinted moisturizers and eye treatment creams. Buy these according to what you can afford. Sometimes the most expensive products contain precious ingredients that bump up the price of the product. Do remember, though, that the cosmetic industry puts great emphasis on packaging: just because a product *looks* attractive it is no indication of quality!

If you have skin that responds badly to stress, and you have a busy lifestyle, then you would be wise to choose hypoallergenic brands. You then minimize the risk of your skin responding badly to a particular product. Treat yourself occasionally to salon treatments – a facial or a cathiodermie, a deep cleansing and nourishing treatment.

'To assess your face shape, pin your hair well back. Stand at arm's length away from a mirror. Close one eye, focussing the other on your face in the mirror. Using an eye pencil, trace the face's outline on the glass. Open both eyes and your face shape will be clear.'

Stephen Glass,
Face Facts

It's worth making time once a week – on a Sunday evening perhaps – to give yourself a mini-facial at home. Deep-cleanse your skin with an exfoliating product and follow with a face mask. This should help counteract the effects of city grime. You could also invest in a collagen or ampoule treatment to revive the skin. There are some wonderful revivers for the skin on the market now to put on pre make-up which act as instant pick-me-ups, tightening and toning the skin.

Always be aware of the detrimental effects of sunlight, and wear a sunscreen when appropriate. If you live healthily, and care for your skin with the right products, it should glow.

Make-Up

'By instantly improving your total look, make-up can give you the confidence to let your attractive inner self take over: that's what I aim to achieve. The women I admire are not great beauties. They are people with their own style, a confident glow and contentment – that's *the very best beautifier of all.'*

Stephen Glass,
Face Facts

A customer once said to me, 'It's all right for you, you have the confidence to wear make-up.' Flabbergasted, I replied, 'I don't have the confidence *not* to.' In our society, make-up is an important part of dressing, and can provide the wearer with a tremendous psychological boost. Make-up can conceal blemishes, play up your best features and disguise your worst, and give your face a 'lift' and colour when you feel completely drained. It's also vital, I think, because women have more delicate skin than men, and foundation along with moisturizer protects the skin on the face from the detrimental effects of the elements.

Make-up should be chosen to enhance the blue-yellow tones in your skin, hair and eyes. If you're predominantly blue-toned then you will find that grey eyeshadow and pink blusher suit you better than the brown eyeshadow and peach blusher a predominantly yellow-toned woman should choose.

While it is true that some colours *do* look better on you than others because of your colouring, you don't have to stick to these suggestions. Make-up colour should also complement your clothes. Depending on how wide a range of colours you have in your clothing wardrobe, you will need different make-up colours to accessorize them. If I, as a sallow-complexioned, yellow-based person (used to wearing orange lipstick) wanted to wear pinks – the more natural province of the blue-toned person – I could. All I would have to do is lighten my skin tone by going for a foundation that has a slightly more pink base to it, by wearing a more blue-pink lipstick and pink blusher, and by wearing a grey eyeshadow instead of a brown one. Somebody who was the opposite to me, with a blue-toned skin, and who wanted to wear a colour more associated with *my* skin tones, would do the reverse: they would choose a more tan-based foundation and blusher, and an orangey lipstick.

It is well worth investing in a make-up lesson from a reputable make-up centre to learn as much as you can about types of make-up and application. Again, as with hair, *your* input is very important; before you buy, talk to the assistant about exactly what you want. If you need several items, then it is worth taking the time to sample several different makes before deciding. An hour's time spent choosing carefully is an investment against time- and money-wasting mistakes.

Make-up expert Stephen Glass recommends that you always keep a make-up bag in your office drawer, containing lipstick and powder and whatever else you consider you need for 'retouching' during the day. This make-up wardrobe can include the basics that you wear every day, plus some glittery extras for evening. The morning session of applying make-up should take no more then 10 minutes.

'Art can perform wonders, which could not, by the uninitiated, be conceived to be within the limits of possibility.'
The Art of Beauty,
Anonymous, 1825

CONCEALER

A light liquid concealer, or a thin cream, can cover dark rings under the eyes without dragging the skin. It can also cover the odd spot or blemish that might erupt. If anything, concealer should be slightly lighter than your foundation, as you want to create light, not shadow. Choose one that dries well rather than one that is creamy. It will stay on better under your foundation.

FOUNDATION

Foundation should be worn over concealer. Always buy foundation by trying it out on your face, rather than the inside of your wrist or back of your hand, where the skin can be a different colour. Check the colour match in natural light, instead of under store lighting which can be deceptive. Drier skin will benefit from a cream foundation, rich in emollients; water-based make-up will last longer on oilier skin. Be aware that when you choose foundation you want to avoid creating a line between the colour of your neck and your face. If you are pale, avoid the trap of choosing foundation to add colour – this will look most unnatural. Instead add colour with blusher.

Foundation goes on most smoothly when it is applied with a sponge (which should be washed daily). If you use finger tips, do make sure that they are clean – a guard against infection and spots.

BLUSHER

Your blusher and lipstick should complement one another in tone. Powder blusher with a good ample brush is easy to apply, but if your skin is very dry, it will benefit from the emollient effect of a cream blusher.

If you take blusher up over the cheekbone beyond the eye and dab a touch on the browbone, then you will create a slimming effect, and give your face life. A matt blusher, in a natural shade, will look best for day wear. Highlighter can lift a face, accentuating the angles and bones. The frosted effect can be rather heavy and obvious, so save it for the evening.

In winter, your skin will be paler, so you will need a stronger blusher; in summer, a golden blusher will accentuate a tan.

POWDER

Fine translucent powder is a must for setting your make-up and making it last. Lightly dusted over your eyelids, it will prevent eyeshadow forming into creases. For 'touching-up' during the day, pressed powder is often a lot more portable. Certain cosmetic houses now make a compact make-up which contains both foundation and powder and which is highly convenient for quick repairs during the day.

EYESHADOW

Eyeshadow should flatter the shape and colour of your eyes, so stick to neutral shades. A wild streak of lurid colour can make you look tarty, even clownish.

Powder eyeshadow lasts better and is less likely to form into creases. Rather than wearing only one colour, it looks far more subtle if you blend two or three. First cover all the eyelid and browbone in a light shade and then blend a darker, more significant colour on the lids. If you want to add a bright or strong colour, then blend it from the inside corner of the eyelid to the middle of the eye. If you have small eyes that you want to make larger, then you should add your darkest shadow at the edges of the eye.

Always blend shadow so that there are no visible hard lines between the shades – the effect you are seeking is a gentle wash of colour. Again, matt eyeshadows are more subtle for day-time wear, and look classier. For evening wear, because the light is dimmer, you can wear frosted eyeshadow and darker colours to greater effect.

Straggly eyebrows can make eyeshadow application uneven: a beauty salon can advise on plucking your eyebrows.

PENCILS

Eye pencils should never drag the delicate skin around the eyes; rubber-tipped pencils, which work like felt-tip pens, make excellent 'smudgers'. To make the eye pencil fast, dip a fine brush into the same colour eyeshadow and go over the pencil line.

If you use pencil on your eyebrows, always carry an eyebrow brush, as powder can often get stuck on the hairs. Dusty eyebrows are hardly conducive to a businesslike appearance.

MASCARA

Avoid mascara that has filaments in it as they can irritate the eyes and make the eyelashes look thick and clogged. If you have small eyes, then use brown mascara on the inner lashes, and black mascara on the outer ones, to make eyes seem wider.

'Most women are not so young as they are painted.'

Max Beerbohm

Coloured mascaras can look cheap, so choose grey, brown or black.

For the sake of the delicate skin around the eyes, choose a mascara that can be removed easily.

LIPSTICK

Lipstick is one of the most important cosmetic aids, adding a clear bright colour that can lift or brighten the face and draw attention away from the eyes if they look tired. The right choice of colour can literally 'make or break' an outfit, so again stick to the yellow/blue tone guidelines outlined in Chapter Four. Paler shades will make small lips seem bigger, and darker shades the reverse.

Pencilling in the lip outline, and using a lip-brush will help the colour last. There are 'long-lasting' lipsticks on the market, but they tend to stain the lips in a very uneven way, and can look messy. Choose your product carefully. There really is no alternative to accepting that you have to retouch your lipstick after drinking coffee, or eating a meal.

Lipstick adds an essential finishing touch to the stylishly dressed businesswoman. For a comparatively small amount of money, you can buy yourself a good lipstick, adding colour to the way you look, and boosting morale.

PERFUME

It's not a good idea to wear overpowering perfume at work, as you want to make an impact through your ability, not your scent. For that reason, I would suggest you wear *eau de toilette* during the day, keeping concentrates and more obtrusive perfumes for the evening.

When I was first thinking about this section, I became aware of just how intrusive many of the recently-introduced perfumes are. I started to think about this quite carefully and eventually decided to launch a new fragrance. My brief to the perfumier was that I wanted a perfume that could be worn day or night, summer or winter, and that was light and natural smelling. It was a revelation to discover just how many ingredients go into a perfume; the proportions in which they are mixed determine the perfume's 'top notes', whether they be woody, floral or musky. It took several months for me to find the particular balance that I liked, and which I hope is the sort of 'classic' perfume that women start to wear in their twenties and then wear until the day they die – the sort of perfume that becomes as individual and particular to them as their signature. I think that a woman should be known by her perfume, and that a scent should appeal to both sexes. Many women feel like I do, totally undressed unless they are wearing perfume.

Recently there has been extensive research into how we

'Stop focussing on your faults, start savouring your plus points – every face has plenty, I promise.'
Stephen Glass,
Face Facts

'Bad taste in clothes is understandable – bad taste in perfume is intolerable.'
James Micklewright,
Perfumier

react to different smells and the findings reveal that the influence of smell is far greater than previously thought. Perhaps this is why some American restaurants have banned the wearing of a particularly brash American perfume, on the grounds that the odour was interfering with the customers' ability to enjoy their food!

Whilst on the subject of smell, it goes without saying that you should always wear a good, adequate deodorant. If you perspire very heavily, then seek medical advice. If you are wearing close-fitting clothes in a warm environment, protect the underarms by stitching in dress shields, circles of fabric that fit under the arms as a 'lining'. Natural fabrics are less likely to cause perspiration.

Use perfume to express your different moods and, if you can afford it, extend your perfume wardrobe to include bath foam, moisturizer and talc, in your favourite brand. Learn to spoil yourself.

NAILS

Most people use their hands to express themselves, particularly when they are enthusiastic about what they are communicating. Your hands are on show as much as your face, and you should attend to their upkeep and maintenance. If your hands are rough, and your nails chewed and grubby, you will send signals out that you are sloppy, do not take care of yourself and are tense. Over-manicured talons with a very bright polish also send out the wrong signals – they suggest that you literally have 'time on your hands' to spend painting and filing your nails.

The well-groomed woman needs hands that look clean and cared for. Always wear rubber gloves to protect your hands when you are doing any sort of manual work, especially if you have problem hands or nails. Protect your nails with a good base coat of nail protector, and then a couple of layers of nail varnish. You can add a daily coat of protector on top. Care for your hands with hand-cream, cuticle cream and by buffing your nails. Your hands show ageing as much as your face does; I keep hand-cream by the side of the bed, and put some on just before I go to sleep, so that it can work overnight.

Your nails look nicest if they match your lipstick colour, but to avoid the necessity of chopping and changing, you could wear a natural colour for business then you won't have to worry about them complementing your outfit.

If your hands are short and stumpy, you might want to wear your nails slightly longer, just enough to elongate the fingers. With badly-textured nails – if they have obvious ridges on the surface, for example – and you want to wear coloured polish; opt for something subtle.

Treat your hands to an occasional manicure. It is especially beneficial to problem hands. At home, you can pamper your hands by soaking them in warm olive oil, particularly helpful during winter months when skin can get rough and chapped.

TEETH

Keep your teeth healthy and sparkling with careful cleaning at home and regular dental checks. Many people mumble or seem reluctant to smile because they are concealing bad teeth. Not only is this spoiling the way you look, but it can also impair their ability to communicate well! So don't take your teeth for granted.

On the delicate subject of bad breath, I always keep some breath freshener tablets in my handbag, for when I've eaten something deliciously spicy or garlicky. They're also useful when in close confines with someone whose breath is not all it should be: I pop a tablet in my mouth and offer my companion one – both tactful and effective.

FEET

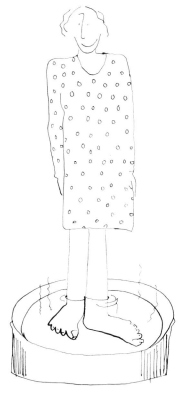

If you are on your feet all day, you will need to pamper them. All too often we ignore foot problems until they become severe, and then the pain registers clearly on our faces.

Choose shoes, tights and socks for comfort as well as style. Most people are aware that shoe comfort is important, but they do not take hosiery into consideration, and fit and comfort are just as important here. If tights are snagging frequently you probably have rough skin on your feet, which needs pumicing away.

There are good products on the market now for soaking feet and massaging them when they are tired, and it is certainly worth having an occasional pedicure. Don't ignore foot problems when they first occur: an early visit to a chiropodist will prevent them developing further.

EXERCISE

For most working women, the greatest demand is to find enough energy to cope with the pressures of running a home and family, and of dealing with a challenging job. For a start, a sensible diet, high in fresh fruit, vegetables and raw food, and drinking plenty of water, will help. Smoking, drinking alcohol and drug taking will not. Respond to the messages that your body gives you: if you always feel tired and are suffering from cold sores or styes, for instance, then you obviously need a good dietary supplement. Don't take vitamins in a haphazard way, though; if you feel your diet is inadequate in some way,

'There is no cosmetic for beauty like happiness.'

Lady Margaret Blessington

then seek the advice of a nutritionist. You will be amazed at how different you feel when you are enjoying a proper diet, based on healthier food.

I believe that exercise and a good diet should help you to relax, and to give you the energy required, and that it should not be an additional stress factor in your life. Experts now acknowledge that physical and mental well-being are inter-dependent, and that regular exercise will produce stress-combating hormones in the body. In my twenties I was fairly sceptical about the benefits of exercise. It took me aback when an expert told me that my dieting was actually depleting my muscle reserve rather than my fat, and I was rapidly converted into an exercise fan! By affecting your metabolic rate, exercise can give you more energy, keep your weight down, and tone up your body. By making you like your body more, exercise can also make you feel more confident and 'body aware'.

However, you need to find an exercise routine that suits your lifestyle. If you are very busy, then an exercise machine in the house, that you can use for 15–20 minutes two or three times a week, could be the answer. The last thing you want to do is to create unrealistic goals for yourself: if you resolve to visit the gym three times a week, then fail to get there because there are too many demands on your time, making you feel disappointed in yourself, you are going to *increase* your stress level instead of reducing it. Exercise should help you cope with pressure, not impose it. Similarly, if you take up a very energetic exercise regime when you are relatively unfit, you will risk increasing your stress level.

Many successful women maintain very high standards for themselves in most areas of their lives, but you should choose exercise for its enjoyment level as well as for achievement. Jog-ging, for example, can cause physical discomfort and certainly will not help the shape of your body if you do not wear an excellent sports bra. The 'feel the burn' school of aerobics has now been discredited to an extent – even Jane Fonda, the high priestess, is advocating 'low impact' aerobics and aerobic walking as preferable alternatives.

Be realistic about the results you expect from any sort of exercise. It must be done regularly – at least three times a week for periods of 20 minutes each time – to show positive results. It cannot change your shape *that* dramatically: you will succeed in redistributing fat, but you cannot alter your skeletal frame, nor drastically change muscle size (unless, of course, you fancy becoming a body-builder). Choose a sport or exer-cise that best helps your shape: if you want to firm up your bust, you are unlikely to do it through jogging, but 50 lengths of breast-stroke three times a week could show good results. Above all, remember to be kind to yourself – you are doing exercise to make you *feel good*!

RELAXATION

The media would sometimes have us believe that every woman should run a perfect beautiful home, and have a well-adjusted family who support and rejoice in her high-earning, high-pressurized career – the Superwoman Syndrome. It is all too easy to fall victim to this and end up achieving a great deal, yet having no time or ability to relax and enjoy a good 'quality of life'. If you are a high-achiever, then you must allow yourself some areas of your life that are strictly non-competitive in which you can *relax*.

Different people find different means of relaxation, and what works for one individual will do nothing for another. Some women find going to the hairdresser relaxing, others find it a nerve-racking experience! More and more people are becoming interested in stress control as the medical profession discover that more and more illnesses are stress-related. Even employers are now beginning to take a more enlightened view, with the most forward thinking introducing stress control and relaxation classes for their employees.

It is most important if you are a busy working woman, and perhaps coping with the demands of running a home and family, that you do something that really helps you to 'switch off' completely. *Make time for it*. Exercise can be relaxation, but sometimes, if you spend your day in high-powered business meetings, then an hour playing with the children can be exhilarating and relaxing, putting your priorities into perspective. If your job is mentally demanding (and few jobs are not), then switching off by doing something manual – tending plants in a peaceful garden, or creatively concocting a meal – can soothe you. When my children were small, I insisted on a quarter of an hour's solitude in the bedroom immediately after I came home from work. I would do perhaps 10 minutes of yoga exercise, then wash my face and slip into a tracksuit. When I emerged I was a far pleasanter individual than if I had gone straight into the kitchen!

You might find you want to study a discipline like meditation, yoga or *tai-chi* to help you relax. If so, enrol in a reputable class to learn the discipline properly. But there are relaxation techniques that you can do by yourself, and which require only a private room. Here are some of them:

If things seem to be going out of control, or you feel anxious or tired about something, then use breathing to regain your composure. Deep breaths, low in the body, will slow down the rate of breathing and allow a steady rate of oxygen to get to the brain. Don't be fooled by the old advice to take a deep breath *in*; what usually happens if we are tense is that we *hold* our breath, creating even more tension in the upper part of the body. Focus instead on breathing *out* slowly and regularly which will also help your fluency and tone in speech.

'There is one thing certain about a well-dressed woman, she has taken trouble. And to take trouble is to strengthen character'.

Robert Lynd,
Journalist and Essayist 1879-1949

You can practise breathing deeply (with your hand on the diaphragm, the sheet of muscle just below the rib cage) most effectively by lying on the floor. Bend your knees up, keeping your feet on the floor, and not too near your bottom. The object is to get the spine as flat and wide on the floor as possible. Breathe easily and deeply with the diaphragm rising as you breathe in, and descending as you breathe out.

Sometimes, clenching and tensing parts of your body can help you to relax (especially useful when you can't sleep). Start at the toes and work upwards through the body. Clench each part – toes, ankles, knees, etc – for a few seconds, and then release it, making sure that it feels completely relaxed. You can even relax your face by tensing and then relaxing it. Some people find this method works very well for them, discovering tension in parts of the body they weren't aware existed!

'Creative visualization' can help you unwind. Imagine yourself in a very pleasant situation – sunning yourself on a beach perhaps, or soaking in a bath of warm scented water. Allow your mind to fill entirely with the picture and sensations of the image, and savour them. This is best done lying down in a darkened room, with your eyes closed, and little distraction.

Treating yourself at a beauty salon is also a great way to unwind. There are many different forms of massage available now, one of the most popular being aromatherapy. This involves massage of your face and body with deeply restorative essential oils. The aromatherapist will chat to you about your health and lifestyle, and try out various oils on you, before diagnosing which oils are appropriate and mixing up her 'prescription'. An oil like lavender, for example, will help you relax and unwind, whilst one like juniper will have more invigorating results.

Shiatsu, an Eastern form of massage based on the pressure points used in acupuncture, is quite a deep treatment. Reflexology, is another Eastern form – in which the feet are massaged – and can be very revealing about the general state of your health. Nerve endings in the feet are associated with various parts of the body, and tenderness in a part of the sole, for instance, can indicate weakness elsewhere in the body. Reflexology is also very relaxing.

Saunas and steam baths can make your skin feel really clean, and help you feel floppily relaxed. If you have dry skin, then opt for steam baths as saunas can have a drying effect. Whilst at the beauty salon you might be tempted to have a solarium treatment: be aware that they can age and dry out the skin. Many salons now offer a 'tanning' service, where the consultant applies self-tanning lotion after exfoliating and moisturizing the skin. If you tend to be heavy-handed at home, this treatment should mean that you are 'streak-free'.

Go for beauty treatments that are pleasant in sensation if you want to relax at the salon. Electrolysis and leg waxing can be painful, so you'll probably prefer to bleach unwanted hair. There is also the risk of bringing veins to the surface when hot wax is poured over the legs.

On a slightly different tack, you can give yourself time to relax and reduce stress by being as organized as you can, and by delegating as much as possible. I keep lists assiduously, even keeping a notebook by the side of the bed; if I have trouble sleeping, then I make a list of what's on my mind. Certainly daily lists, with things to do and the time allocated to them, are indispensable.

If you're irritable a great deal of the time because of over-load, then it could be worth sacrificing your fortnight in Italy for a cleaning lady three hours a week. Save your time and energy by having food delivered, or if you can afford it, get a catering company in to cook for your dinner parties. Get into the habit of thinking about what exactly makes life easier for you. You are not being selfish, because if you're happy and feel that you are on top of life, then your immediate family will also reap the benefits of your good humour!

Every eight weeks or so, give yourself what's been called a 'mental health day' – a day when you do exactly what you want, be it visiting an art gallery or having a top-to-toe beauty treatment. This relaxation day should be sacred to you, and it should sustain you through difficult, hectic days in between.

POISE AND POSTURE

'Poise' is an old-fashioned word, and one we don't hear used much – probably because it is a quality difficult to achieve in our tornado-paced world. It implies a serenity and an ability to cope that are not implicit in the word 'confidence'; it comes from knowing yourself, both vices and virtues, and from a healthy dose of self-esteem.

So, how do you appear 'poised'? Well, good posture will con-tribute enormously. You could put a woman in the most won-derfully tailored suit, but if her shoulders are rounded and her stance apologetic, she will never look effective. Good posture means the neck and head are in natural alignment with the rest of the body, a position in which the head can be nodded easily, and the shoulders are relaxed. Women often distort their pos-ture by rounding their shoulders (an apology for a generous bust), or by desperately sucking in their tummy muscles, thrusting the upper part of their bodies forwards. Sometimes, small women thrust their chins upwards in an attempt to appear taller, throwing the head out of alignment. We often take tension in the shoulders and neck, and end up with a head continually thrust forwards, and hunched-up shoulders.

'A woman has a real disadvantage. It is too bad that women have to age like men, because we are treated equally. You have fat, sloppy men but they get away with it. They are millionaires and everyone treats them with respect. When a millionairess happens to be fat and sloppy no one remembers that she is a self-made, capable person. What they do remember is that she is fat and sloppy!

Leah Hertz,
from *The Business Amazons*

(Massage can help relax these areas, as can gently rotating the shoulders and nodding the head to free the neck.) Habitually bad posture takes its toll on the spine, often causing backache and that all-too-familiar hump at the base of the neck which can appear as women get older. If you have a bad postural problem, then it could be worth investing in a course of Alexander Technique lessons, which will help you find correct and comfortable physical alignment, and contribute to your sense of well-being.

Poise also reveals itself in the way you move and sit, and the lack of nervous mannerisms. You look 'poised' when your energy is focused and under control, so avoid hair twiddling, playing with your chin, nails or jewellery. (Jerky, nervous movements like these make others around you nervous too.) When you sit, allow the back of your chair to take the weight, with your hands resting gently in your lap; don't lean anxiously forward, with your arms crossed in a defensive position. In fact, you are *less* likely to be verbally attacked in a business meeting if you look open and receptive.

Fortunately, there are experts today who specialize in every area of self-presentation. If you feel for some reason that you are lacking poise, then seek advice about tackling the problem. By 'knowing yourself' and by not imposing unrealistic expectations upon yourself, you can look and feel happy and fulfilled.

'All well and good, this advice,' you may think, 'but when do I have time to put it all into practice?' To appear well-groomed and to cope with a busy lifestyle, you must establish a routine. Habit governs most of what we do, from the soap powder we buy to the food that we eat, so to improve your 'total look', you must introduce new habits into a regular routine.

Gradually phase in new routines so that they become easy to assimilate in your lifestyle. One month you might start having a regular manicure; the following month you could decide to add eyeshadow or blusher to the limited range of cosmetics that you apply daily; you might have to forego one or two hours at home to fit in an exercise or relaxation class. Try to think of ways in which you could achieve two things at once when pampering yourself: give yourself a manicure or pedicure while sitting with a face mask on; condition your hair, wrapping it in a plastic bag or a shower-cap, while doing your 20 minutes of floor exercises.

There is absolutely no need to feel guilty, self-obsessed or frivolous – you are improving your self-esteem, the way others see you, and consequently your efficiency and quality of life.

CHAPTER TEN

SPECIAL OCCASIONS

Depending on the job you have, for some of you travel will not be a 'special occasion' but something done on a frequent basis. In this case, I expect your own experience will have provided you with sound practical guidelines. Some of you will dread travelling, however, because you never feel that you are organized about your packing or know what to take. In this chapter, therefore, I aim to help you realize that if you are adequately prepared, travelling need not seem such a nightmare. (And even the seasoned traveller might learn a tip or two!)

Company outings can be particularly difficult 'special occasions' to dress for as you need to present a businesslike image but also one that is more glamorous than your day-to-day look. Many women tend to err on one side or the other; anxious to project professionalism, they end up looking severe or drab, or they project such a glamorous image that their colleagues fail to recognize them!

Pregnancy, is of course a very 'special occasion' and one which more and more women are choosing to work through, at least until the last couple of months. Fortunately, with the diversity of styles that are now in fashion every season, it is always possible to find stylish outfits in a 'baggy look' that need not necessarily come from specialist maternity wear shops.

All these special occasions can be stressful in their own ways, and being worried about not being appropriately dressed or looking as good as you normally do will only add to the strain. I hope this chapter will make these instances easier to cope with.

TRAVELLING ON BUSINESS

If you travel away regularly on business, as I do, packing can become a chore that is often dreaded and done in a rush.

Unlike packing to go away on holiday, when you can enjoy choosing what clothes to wear for relaxation, packing for business means that efficiency and an immaculate appearance have to be your main priorities.

LUGGAGE

One of the first considerations should be your luggage. It is often more important than you think, especially when you are being met the other end by a business colleague. Much as we hate to admit it, you are judged as much by what you carry as by what you wear. Hotel porters, for instance, often treat you quite differently if you have good luggage rather than clothes bulging out of a tattered case. Presumably if you look expensive and the luggage enhances the hotel foyer, it makes you a prestigious guest (you might even, dare I say it, be a good bet for large tips).

I like toughened canvas luggage; it is light and hard-wearing. You can build up a luggage 'wardrobe', starting off with a medium-sized suitcase, then adding a piece of hand luggage, then perhaps a suit-carrier bag. Canvas luggage can have an attractive leather trim and if you buy it with a frame it will protect your clothes well. Although good luggage is expensive, it should last many years, and you will have time to build up a good collection – it is a long-term investment. Cheap luggage, on the other hand, will not stand much wear and tear or batterings in the holds of aeroplanes.

Fibreglass suitcases are hard-wearing and substantial. They often come with sets of wheels, which are useful if you have to walk a long way at an airport. Always label your luggage very carefully, and if you have a suitcase that is a popular make, then add a distinguishing mark, with either a sticker or some tape. There is nothing worse after a long journey than discovering that your luggage has inadvertently been taken by somebody else who mistook it for their own.

The weight of the empty luggage should always be taken into consideration before buying; you don't want to buy something that you have difficulty lifting when full.

PACKING

For a business trip, build your wardrobe around a basic, like black court shoes which go with your black briefcase. If you are going on four-day business trip, travelling on two of the days, and attending a conference on the other two, then you could pack two suits which go with the shoes and briefcase. Add a couple of sweaters or T-shirts and blouses, depending on the time of year, and some jewellery to 'dress up' the suits in the evening, and you have a comprehensive wardrobe. A knitted two-piece or dress is very useful too and takes up little space.

'I've always been interested in a woman who is busy, who travels, who is confident with her image and who doesn't buy extravagant evening-wear but will dress up daywear for night. Six years ago women were just beginning to live like that, it was a New York situation. Now the myth is becoming a fact, internationally, not just in New York City.'

Michael Kors,
Fashion Designer

HOW TO USE YOUR TRAVEL WARDROBE.

Travelling Day 1
Wear suit A with sweater and coat

Conference Day 2
Wear suit B with sweater or good quality T-shirt in day, suit A in evening with a different blouse and different jewellery

Conference Day 3
Wear suit A in day, adding a scarf instead of jewellery, and suit B in evening with different blouse to Day 2 and different jewellery (perhaps more glittery)

Travelling Day 4
Wear suit B with T-shirt and coat

If this arrangement seems rather restricting, consider that you could take six different tops, ranging from blouse to sweater to T-shirt, and different jewellery and make-up. These take up little space, are not too heavy, and can give you a new look every time that you change. A scarf here would be a useful accessory; it's light to pack and very versatile.

Lightweight wools travel well and creases drop out quickly. In summer, if you decide to take a linen suit, take a portable steam iron with you, or check that the hotel has a good pressing facility. It's a good idea to plan to get your clothes cleaned just before you go away, then you can pack them in the cleaner's polythene bags – these are more efficient than tissue paper in keeping creases at bay.

Always put tailored clothes at the bottom of the suitcase. (Never carry tailored clothes in a soft frameless bag – they will arrive very crumpled.) When folding a jacket, button it up, fold it in two across the body, revers facing you, and bring the arms across the chest. Use tissue paper or polythene to pad any obvious places where creasing will occur, like the shoulders and revers. Apply the same principle to dresses, shirts and trousers. Bear in mind that shoes, T-shirts, lingerie and silk pleated skirts can go round the edges and are far less likely to crease if they are rolled rather than folded. Keep shoes in bags; many shoe-makers now give you bags when you buy shoes, so keep them for travelling. Using soft, light-weight shoe trees is useful to protect shape.

Avoid any risk of spillage on your clothes by carrying your wash-bag as hand luggage or wrapping it in a large freezer bag, tightly secured. Because I do a lot of travelling, I keep a 'duplicate' wash-bag, with a set of small bottles containing all my favourite skin-care products, ready for me to travel at a moment's notice. If it's in my hand luggage, then I can freshen up en route.

'The important thing about a suit, and I wear them a lot, is that when you take your jacket off, it should look just as smart. I want clothes that are elegant and professional and, of course, feminine... that's highly important.'
Suzanna Hammond
Managing Director,
Ogilvy & Mather PR

Most hotels provide hair-dryers, but if you are particularly attached to yours, then remember to take an adaptor plug if you are going abroad. There are now plugs available, which adapt to American and European voltages. A portable steamer, with a clothes brush attachment, can be very useful. I always take shoe creams, because although hotels usually provide shoe-shine, they rarely provide creams in the right colours. A mini-repair kit, with safety-pins, needles and thread is useful, as are spare pairs of tights, and if you are travelling in Britain – a portable umbrella!

TRAVEL TIPS

Comfort needs to be the main priority when choosing what to wear when to travel. Many women find tracksuits snug and relaxing to wear on long train trips or air flights. The only disadvantage, in my experience, is that you can feel as though you are wearing pyjamas when you reach your destination! Cotton jersey is very comfortable, and I prefer to wear a cotton jersey top and skirt, that I can throw a jacket over, when I arrive. Any sort of wool or cotton 'knits' will be fairly crease-resistant.

If you want to take a coat on a trip, do consider how much you will wear it. A heavy overcoat can be a real burden when you are rushing from airport to taxi to hotel. Even in quite cold climates, the amount of time you actually spend outside braving the elements can be very small. A fur coat is not only very heavy, but a security risk on a long trip. For warmth, I'd suggest you take an extra thick layer, a soft sweater perhaps to pop over your cotton jersey top and under your jacket, for outside wear. Layers of clothing keep you warmer anyway; a soft sweater or large scarf gives you something that you can snuggle up in and feel quite cosy. If you're changing climate zones, a pretty thermal vest can be very useful.

I always take a spare, cheap purse with me when I go abroad. I then transfer the currency of the country I am visiting into my usual purse, and store my English money in the spare, ready for my return the other end. This I find a particularly useful device for maintaining good relations with cab drivers!

You might like to include in your luggage a special treatment – a face mask, for example – which you might have more time for at the end of a busy day. I also carry an exercise gadget so that I can keep up a routine whilst away. A relaxing bath oil is also invaluable. To avoid tightness and dryness on your face due to the dehydrating effects of a long journey, use a special preparation available for this purpose. When I'm feeling stale on a flight, I always find that brushing my teeth revives me.

To reduce the effects of jet lag on the day of my return I set my watch to British time on waking and eat accordingly. If I were flying from America to Britain, I'd lunch in the morning and have my equivalent of an evening meal in the early after-

'When visiting hotels, it's wrong to assume that someone will always whip-up an ironing board when you need it – even in the most expensive hotels they don't – so look for fabrics that travel well and come straight out of the suitcase looking like a million dollars.'
Glenys Roberts,
Writer and Newspaper Columnist

noon. Early evening I would just have a light snack. This system minimizes the effects of air travel on my 'body clock'. Some airlines are flexible in their catering arrangements and will readily provide a vegetarian meal or a plate of fruit if asked. You will feel much better after a long flight if you avoid alcohol, drink plenty of water and eat fruit, to keep your blood sugar level up.

To help you sleep on a flight take an eye mask, and an inflatable neck cushion. These are now available from chemists' and airline shops. Half-inflated, they are wonderfully comfortable and make snoozing easy.

Air travel can be stressful and tiring, so go as comfortably as you can afford. You might think that it's a needless extravagance to travel business class, but your performance at the other end will undoubtedly benefit from the extra rest you will have got. In travel, as in all things, be kind to yourself!

COMPANY ENTERTAINING

These days, more and more companies combine business with social or leisure activities, be it a night at the opera or a sailing weekend aboard the company yacht.

If your work does involve a great deal of work-related socializing, then choose at least one suit that is not too severely cut and can be worn with a dressy silk shirt or T-shirt. This should see you through cocktail parties and dinner engagements immediately after work. But, to expand the ideas outlined in the capsule wardrobe, your most useful investment would be a tailored evening jacket, either blazer style or collarless, in a glittery or textured fabric. This still denotes structure and formality in your style, but looks more glamorous. It is also a godsend if you are unsure as to how dressy you should look; you can have something plain underneath if you are in fear of over-dressing, and something dressy and revealing if you think that you might be in danger of underplaying the situation.

For more formal occasions, you can look glamorous, but do try to avoid anything overtly revealing that could be read as vulgar. Company dinners can be a strain for partners of employees, but don't be tempted to dress 'down', whichever category you belong in. If you are a partner you should do your husband or wife credit: there is nothing quite so humiliating as having an eye cast over you which is saying, '... and that insignificant person is his/her partner?' Meeting someone's partner is like meeting a first boyfriend's parents – a great deal is explained and you never see the person in quite the same light again!

Modern classics from your capsule wardrobe should equip you for more casual company activities. Your check jacket can be accessorized with well-cut gabardine or cotton trousers or jeans. A cream linen suit, which, in the particular season of the time of writing, would have a long jacket and shortish skirt, would equip you for occasions like Henley, Ascot or Wimbledon. A navy suit jacket, worn with jeans and deck-shoes, could provide the basis for your wardrobe at a sailing week. If it is important that you look smart and retain your status at casual events, then your best investments would be a denim suit and a good leather jacket. These are adaptable and great examples of modern classics in casual dressing.

PREGNANCY

It can be a problem for the businesswoman to find appropriate pregnancy wear. Many specialist shops tend to stock rather frilly frocks that look 'little girly' and which are not appropriate for work. The best solution seems to be to buy dresses a couple of sizes larger and have them altered if necessary. So if you are a size 10, then you'd buy a size 14. You could always belt the dress after you'd had the baby, though in my experience, most women have had so much wear out of their maternity dresses that they never want to see the garments again!

The best style of dress is a straight roomy cut that falls from a yoke. Avoid button-through styles as they will tend to pop open. An interesting collar line and pretty jewellery will draw attention to your face rather than your bulk. Be aware when you buy pregnancy clothing that you can expand both forwards and backwards, and that the garment should allow for this. In summer, you will feel hotter than you do normally, so go for very light-weight materials.

Rather than buying a coat in the winter, choose a lined trenchcoat which is roomy, and can be belted post-pregnancy. A large, loose-fitting jacket can be useful too. Make sure that your clothes do not need to be worn with high heels, as these will be uncomfortable. Take advice as to whether you need to wear support tights to prevent varicose veins.

Accept that, proportionately, you will look larger than you ever have before. Small accessories and little details in your clothes will look unbalanced with your size. Go for roomy bags and obvious jewellery. It is also important, I think, to enjoy your appearance whilst you are pregnant, and you should cherish your body and baby by eating sensibly, and pampering yourself with the creams and lotions especially designed for pregnant women. Gentle exercise – swimming or walking – will also keep you fit and help your return to your former svelte shape.

After the birth, you may need to wear clothes that are still a size bigger than you were before conception. If you're dying to buy yourself something new, then choose a couple of reasonably priced, not too fitted, dresses.

CHAPTER ELEVEN

SHOPPING

Very often we buy clothes impulsively and with little fore-thought. For the busy woman, shopping can be a night-mare of rushing from shop to shop desperately looking for something suitable. She usually ends up buying for short-term use only! In this chapter I intend to point out some of the hazards and pitfalls of shopping, explain how the retail trade works, and help you to develop a few essential 'shopping skills'.

'It's important to tune in to the organization you're working for. Your dress should never distract from how you operate. In some professions – say, television – being individualistic is more the norm.'

Wendy Pritchard,
Management Consultant

SOME SHOPPING MISTAKES

The most common mistake – is going shopping without a list. Because I advocate buying fewer clothes of higher quality, cost, planning and analysis beforehand are vital. Carry your wardrobe 'list' (see page 50) in your wallet and use it whenever you shop. With all its details of cut, cloth and colour – and after a quick glance at the chart below – you should never again be tempted to make unwise purchases.

CUT, CLOTH AND COLOUR CHECKLIST

CUT	CLOTH	COLOUR
Does it fit me?	Is the weight appropriate for the temperature in which I work/travel/socialize?	How does it fit in with the rest of my wardrobe?
How does it move?		Does it suit me?
How does the shape compare with mine?		Will I get tired with it?
	Does it feel soft or stiff?	Will it show dirt easily?
Is the cut soft or sharp?	How does it fit in with other fabrics in my wardrobe?	Will it be difficult to match?
Do the details show a strong fashion influence?		Is it a particularly strong fashion colour?
	Is it easily cleaned?	
Can it be altered?	Does it need to be lined?	Do I feel good in it?
Will it be wearable in two years' time?	Will it crease easily?	Will I need to buy new accessories as well?
Do I feel comfortable in it?	How do I care for it?	

Many women tend to buy clothes on impulse when they need cheering up, and horrific mistakes can be made. If you're impulsive in this way, acknowledge the tendency, and rather than splashing out on a garment that will make you feel guilty afterwards, buy yourself some make-up or perfume that is less of an extravagance. Even a good hair-conditioning treatment or a bottle of scented body lotion can give you a much needed boost, when a expensive blouse that you only wear once would be sheer folly. Remember the cost-per-wear theory, and if you use that body lotion for six months, it has proved itself a far more economical investment than the once-worn blouse. Save your clothes shopping for a time when you feel calm, logical and happy!

Newspapers and magazines sometimes influence us to buy clothes that we should not. Every woman's magazine has a fashion section, as do most newspapers, and the clothes that they show are invariably worn by professional models who tend to be very tall, very thin and, often, very young. They bear little resemblance to the majority of us, and what they look good in will not necessarily look good on the average – even the *above* average – woman. If you relied on the fashion pages to analyse the range available in the shops, you could end up believing that when a 'new look' takes off, that it is the only one available. Remember that the media always seeks the sensational, and a 'new look' can happily fill column inches. Realism, however, is seldom newsworthy, and the shops still stocking realistic clothes are not always likely to be the ones to get exposure. Consider, too, that fashion companies often use PRs to get themselves publicity, and that being written about is not necessarily a recommendation of quality. I feel, therefore, that most media fashion coverage doesn't help the working woman choose clothes that suit her as an *individual*. What you *can* learn from the good fashion pages is how to put a 'look' together, and what accessories work best with different styles of clothing.

Most clothes shops gear themselves to a selling to a particular sort of customer, described in terms of age, income and quality preference.

So do be prepared, when you walk into a good quality clothes shop, for them to make instant judgements about you. If you look a mess, the sales people might just ignore you – or they may even follow you around thinking you're a shop lifter, a horrible feeling! You don't have to dress up to the nines, but if you make yourself look as presentable as possible, they'll know you are a serious customer. If you think this might happen, and want to *pre-empt* that judgement, you can simply walk in and ask for advice immediately. You may find it difficult – many people dislike displaying that lack of confidence – but it could be absolutely the best thing to do.

'Don't succumb to colours because they happen to be "in". It's far better to look terrific than fashionable.'
Stephen Glass,
Face Facts

Individual shops also have a certain 'style', and you need to find the style that suits you. The advice in Chapter Four, and elsewhere in the book, should be a good starting point. A friend can look terrific in a garment from a particular shop, but if she is a blonde, romantic looking 5′ 7″ sylph and you are a curvy, vivacious 5′3″ brunette, there is a strong likelihood that the stockists' style may not suit you!

Fashion shops set out to seduce the potential purchaser to part with money, and in recent years 'lifestyle' shops such as Laura Ashley and Next have boomed. The idea behind these shops is most attractive to busy people – you enter an emporium crammed with a range of goods that suit your lifestyle, from clothes to cutlery, all chosen tastefully. You can satisfy a lifestyle image in your home and the way you dress, be it for rustic nostalgia or high-tech yuppiedom. This is fine if you crave that certain image, but it falls considerably short when catering for the individualist. I believe that most successful women in business are strongly individual – they need to be to have got where they are – so these shops should only be used for expediency. If you want to stand out in the way you present yourself, seek clothing expression elsewhere.

Being uncertain about what suits you or what you want is a major shopping mistake, and you can fall victim to the perils of the forceful sales person. If you feel that you are being persuaded to buy something against your better judgement, then tell the sales person that you would like to think about it and you'll call her or return early the next day. Her reaction to this should be a barometer as to her integrity. If she takes issue with you, then you can suspect that you are being persuaded to buy something that does not really suit you. If she's amenable, then her judgement and encouragement are probably sound. However, if you've absorbed the lessons of this book, you should be more confident in your own instincts. Whether she's forceful or not, always be honest with the sales person. If she says that you look marvellous in a garment, but you can't see it, then tell her so. Ask her to be more precise about cut, cloth, colour, fit etc., countering with your own reactions. Shopping is a two-way process and involves a two-way communication between customer and sales person. It would be a mistake to grumble if your input had not been entirely truthful.

Finally, never buy clothes when you are in a hurry. This is when the greatest mistakes can be made. Take time to try the garments on, and never let yourself be hurried by a sales person. Move about in the garment as you would when wearing it at home or at work. If you sit a lot, then sit in the clothes in the shop to ensure they are comfortable. Look at yourself in the mirrors from all angles, and ask for another if necessary to see back and sides properly. Only when *you* are absolutely sure, should you say 'yes'.

'Why do fashions in clothes change? Because, really, we ourselves change in the slow metamorphoses of time. If we imagine ourselves now in the clothes we wore six years ago, we shall see that it is impossible. We are, in some ways, different persons now, and our clothes express our different personality.'
D. H. Lawrence.
Writer, 1885-1930

CHOOSING SHOPS

When going clothes shopping, there are roughly four different types of shop to choose from – designer boutiques, middle-price chain shops, department stores and high-street stores. Each type has its 'style' and its devoted customers, and the following brief descriptions should help you to choose what would be best for you. You'll gather *my* views on this quite quickly!

DESIGNER BOUTIQUES

These are the top end of the market, and if you shop in one you can expect prices to be high. Some designer shops carry goods that are exclusively made by one designer, but I would not advocate a great deal of shopping there unless you want to look 'labelled'. You can expect greater choice in a shop that carries several labels.

If you want to buy designer clothes, then comb the market to find out just who designs for your lifestyle. Fashion magazines and advertisements can be useful in this respect. In my opinion, some designers have been 'hyped' to a level that is way out of proportion to their talent. The best designers, however, have often been around for years and have a faithful following. Their clothes will not date and, if looked after, should last for years. I prefer Italian design for women in business – the cutting and cloth tend to be of excellent quality.

A suit from a quality designer shop will never be cheap, and if you really cannot afford such an investment, I would still urge you to visit these shops even if only to *study* the clothes. Learn what makes their stock such high quality in terms of cut, cloth and colour and use this knowledge to discriminate when you are shopping at a cheaper level. Be warned, though, that 'quality' is highly addictive, and you could decide to buy one designer outfit for a season rather than several cheaper ones. I suggest that as soon as you are in an income bracket where you can afford to do this, you should.

Browsing in designer shops can give a fascinating insight into how the fashion industry works. If you pop into a high-street store immediately afterwards, you will, in all probability, see their adapted versions of the designers' trends. To keep costs down, however, the high-street versions will have been mass-produced in cheaper fabrics, and cut and cloth might well be incompatible. A figure-skimming number, skilfully cut by the designer in a soft wool jersey, will have been cut in a more extreme way and in a cheaper fabric won't work at all as the designer intended.

MIDDLE-PRICE CHAINS

This group ranges from companies that have four or five shops in a capital city, to nationwide chains that have a hundred or so

'Women are not dolls to be dressed by designers; I would ask them, have you no brains? Yes, you have intelligence. Then please express that intelligence in dressing yourself.'

Jean Patou,
from *Patou*, Meredith Etherington Smith

outlets. They tend to create an image that appeals to the younger end of the market, and the clothes show strong fashion trend influence. Often these shops will stock clothes in a restricted colour range with two or three colours dominating each season. This can make matching garments difficult, unless you buy complete outfits from the shops. You should also bear in mind that the chain will produce many versions of the same garment.

Some of these shops will also carry more exclusive and therefore expensive garments. These are likely to show strong fashion influences as well.

DEPARTMENT STORES
In my opinion, there is a major drawback in shopping in chain and department stores. Unlike smaller shops, which are often owner-managed, chain and department stores often employ buyers who have little contact with the public, as they are rarely on the shop floor. As a result, they lack the continual input from customers that some smaller shops have – and which is so vital for true success.

However, for the shopper who wishes to remain anonymous, then department stores are a boon. Because these shops are designed to get as many customers as possible into them, you are unlikely to receive too much attention from a sales person. Of course, there are plusses to department store shopping in that everything is housed under one roof. But if it's individual attention you're after, then you would be wiser to clothes shop somewhere smaller.

HIGH-STREET CHAINS
In that they produce thousands of the same garment at relatively low cost and reduced quality, these do not have great appeal for many women in business. They can be useful for lingerie, perhaps.

IDENTIFYING A 'GOOD' SHOP
First of all, the unsuspecting customer needs to be aware that not all the fashion industry's practices are above reproach. Did you know, for instance, that some shops use mirrors with a slimming effect, or that some chains buy an outfit solely 'for the press', to attract press coverage? Neither is media coverage of shops invariably honest or impartial, so be discriminating about the fashion advice that you read. Word of mouth, from someone whose opinion you trust (and whom you think dresses well), is usually the best recommendation. Also, new shops often take a while to establish their style and determine exactly what sort of customer they appeal to, so if you want

'How men hate waiting while the wives shop for clothes and trinkets, how women hate waiting, often for much of their lives, while their husbands shop for fame and glory.'
Thomas Szasz,
The Second Sin

reliable advice you are better off going to a shop which has already carved out a niche for itself, and which understands its customers.

This is going to upset some people, but I think that capital city shops offer a far greater selection than those in the suburbs. If you are contemplating a major refit of your wardrobe, then you should go to a major city to do it. Unlike France and Italy, where designers deliver to smaller cities like Lyons and Nice or Bologna and Florence, many designer clothes are not available outside the capitals in Britain, America or Australia. British provincial shops that stock collections, for instance, are likely to be six months behind their London counterparts. This is because of the cosmopolitan nature of London, where shop-owners are exposed to feedback from an international clientele. This is not to say that women who live outside capital cities are less stylish than their metropolitan cousins, but I would suggest that any woman who takes her appearance seriously should make at least one annual shopping trip to the city where she will find most choice and possibly more cosmopolitan and aware sales assistants.

Good shop-owners have to give careful consideration to the customers they wish to attract, and the amount of money they will spend. Too wide a dichotomy in prices is confusing to the customer, so shops that carry a very wide price range of clothes should be avoided. There is no escaping the fact that each of us falls into a particular income bracket – acknowledge this, and find the shop that best suits your pocket. I must repeat here, too, my assertion that expensive clothes are not necessarily *good* clothes. You could pay an awful lot of money for a suit that might be of good quality and has some fine workmanship in its detail, yet it could be in very poor taste. These expensive gimmicky clothes are often the ones that are hyped by the press.

A good shop must do alterations. Very few women are lucky enough to find garments that fit them exactly, and I almost regard a sale as a 'first fitting' before the necessary small alterations are made. Skirts and sleeves can be shortened or lengthened, waists and hips can be let out or, more easily taken in. Even the bust can be taken in or let out. Many shops, because they do not have an alterations facility, try to persuade the customer that a garment which is ill-fitting in fact fits well. (Beware those unscrupulous sales people who will persuade you that something fits by tucking in the waist and quickly pinning it, or suggesting that too-long sleeves are worn rolled up.) If you are looking for a good fit, you can easily end up in despair at the irregularities in your shape. Take heart, and remember that the garment is made in a fixed shape, with a view to it fitting many different bodies. There is absolutely no reason why you should expect clothes to fit your body perfectly, and a

'Fashion is a form of ugliness so intolerable that we have to alter it every six months.'
Oscar Wilde,
Writer, 1854–1900

skilled alterations person will be able almost totally to remake a garment. Of course, cost is a factor in all this and extensive alteration to an already expensive suit could prove prohibitive. If you really like something, though, and want to feel completely comfortable in it, then it is well worth taking the time and spending the money to get it altered.

(Sizing varies enormously from manufacturer to manufacturer anyway, so you should never go shopping seeing yourself rigidly as one size. Many labels are deceptive, and one designer might call you a size 12, another a size 10. Avoid discounting garments because they don't seem to be your size – you could have a pleasant surprise when you try them on! We re-size most clothes that we bring in to Wardrobe, by studying them closely and measuring them.)

A good shop should have good sales people. I like to employ women who have not worked in a fashion shop before, because in Britain the retail trade has such a bad reputation and many sales people have a negative attitude towards their work, through previous bad experience. Britain is not yet as service-orientated as France, Italy and America, and sales people are not particularly well paid. Selling, however, is an important talent, and should be regarded as a skill to be proud of. A good sales person is one who can guide and make constructive suggestions to her customers, rather than one who is in selling because she thinks she can't do anything else. If you are ever confronted with that shopper's nightmare – a pushy sales person who is out to earn her commission at any cost to the customer – then make your excuses and leave, or find another sales person who is more considerate.

The perfect sales person should be an amateur psychologist, who can tune in fairly rapidly to you and your lifestyle, and she should have a good sense of style, proportion and colour. She should be able to make a quick assessment of your shape and be able to suggest items from her stock that will suit you. Knowledge of stock is a most important aspect of skilled selling, and that stock should include accessories and shoes that add those important finishing touches to any outfit.

The ambiance and facilities a shop offers are enormously important too. Shop design has recently become increasingly significant, and many companies are employing top designers and architects to refurbish their interiors. The design of the shop gives a strong indication as to whom they think their customers are, and to the taste of the owners. (Thankfully, the fashion for harsh black and chrome, making shops look more like art galleries, seems to be dying out.) You should not be *too* aware of a shop interior, however; after all, you've gone in to look at goods, not the walls, and the ambiance should be one that encourages a relaxing browse.

Loud relentless music has the opposite effect on me, distrac-

'The history of the world is largely the history of dress. It is the most illuminating of records and tells its tale with a candour and completeness which no chronicle can surpass.'

Agnes Rippler,
Americans and Others

ting me completely. I can see that it could increase the excitement of shopping, the 'thrill of the chase' as it were, but it often seems to make the sales staff edgy as well, especially when they have to shout at the customers in order to be heard!

In a good shop, lighting should be strategically placed so that you can see the clothes clearly. In fact, you should always look at clothes in natural light, as artificial lighting can be so deceptive: that blue skirt you are thinking of buying could easily be transformed into a deep aqua once you get it outside. If the changing rooms are not adequately lit, then go into the main shop to look in the mirror. The changing rooms themselves should be separate, and if they are very small and you feel cramped, then I'd ask the sales person if they have anywhere bigger for you to change. Few women like communal changing rooms: how can you make a proper decision when you're surrounded by jostling bodies in various stages of undress? There should be plenty of mirrors too in the changing rooms so that you can look at yourself from all angles. (You are not always going to be looked at face on.) If you suspect that a mirror is creating a slimming illusion, then look around to find a more honest reflection in another mirror.

Good shop-keepers will care about their stock and should keep chiffon scarves available so that you can cover your face when putting clothes on, thus minimizing the risk of getting make-up on them. I suggest you always carry a scarf for this purpose when you shop, as some places are not that fastidious about washing their scarves regularly. Of course, it's to the shop's detriment if you do soil a garment, but you will feel unhappy about it too, especially if you want to buy the garment!

When to Shop

For some women, browsing in shops is very relaxing, and shopping is almost a hobby. Many more of us would like to have lots of time to shop, but end up doing it in a rushed and harassed state of mind. This, as I already mentioned, is one of the most basic shopping mistakes. You will find shopping a more pleasant experience if you consider the best times to go – both for yourself and for the shops. For instance, the best 'spiritual' time to go is when you feel positive about yourself; if you are feeling negative, you won't be satisfied with anything.

At certain times of the year shops have the widest possible selection of stock, so if you can schedule major shopping trips to coincide with these periods – around February, March and September – it will make choices easier for you. There is nothing quite so frustrating as deciding that you want to buy a new suit, and finding all the shops at the tail end of their sales, with very little to offer.

'Only the rich can afford to buy fashion clothes, because they can replace them every season.'
Amanda Williams,
Restaurant Manager

To assemble a complete outfit, it is often necessary to visit several shops, which is very time-consuming if you do it on a piecemeal basis. (Mail-order shopping is booming as a result, though this has severe disadvantages for women to whom good fit and quality of cut and cloth are important.) You can use your time much more effectively in shopping by opting to have a couple of major buying sessions a year, when you get large items and complete outfits, rather than a steady 'dribble' of purchasing throughout the year. And if you are spending a lot of time scouring a small town for exactly what you want, then you could be very much better off making that couple of buying trips to a large city every year. A good opportunity to combine pleasure with the business of self-promotion too!

Always avoid lunchtimes and Saturdays, when shops are at their busiest. I like shopping in the morning, when the sales staff are more fresh and (one hopes) helpful. If you are very busy yourself, then you might care to shop by appointment – phoning up the shop in advance to tell them what you are look-ing for, so they can think about your requirements beforehand. Some shops will stay open late if you have made an appoint-ment, making your 'out of hours' shopping all the easier.

If you *hate* shopping and choose to use a personalized shop-ping service – to let someone do your shopping *for* you – take care to use a recommended expert, rather than an amateur who has been told that they have good taste and see it as a 'little business'. A proper shopping expert needs to have had considerable experience in evaluating proportion and the quality of garments, and we often find ourselves at Wardrobe picking up the pieces!

Sales Shopping

Shops hold sales to help their cash flow, not as a bean-feast for the customers. It is very easy, at sale time, to be carried forth on a wave of adrenalin at the excitement of getting goods cheaply. The shrewd sales shopper goes to a shop where she knows the stock, to buy something that she has wanted, but not pre-viously been able to afford. The mistakes to avoid are thinking about a new fashion garment all season, then succumbing to it 'because it was cheap in the sale' and thereafter never wearing it, and buying things that you don't need just because they are reduced. Really scan your wardrobe list before you go to the sales.

Classic clothes, handbags and accessories can be good in sales buys. The practice of shops 'buying in' for sales is now dying out, and goods are usually marked as such. (They're not usually a good buy anyway, as the fact that they have been 'bought in' usually means that someone else has failed to sell them first.)

IT WAS IN THE SALE.

A good idea is to ask your favourite shop to mail you about the first day of their sale. More often than not there is a preview day for mailing-list customers.

How the Retail Business Works

Very few customers know how the retail trade works – just how far in advance the range of clothes for a season is chosen, for instance – so I think some facts will be most useful in helping you refine your shopping skills.

It might be easiest to describe what is happening at the time of writing – the beginning of March 1988. I am going to the Milan collections and will buy clothes for the winter of 1988–89. This 'buy' has to happen early, because at the more expensive end of the market fabric manufacturers only produce to order. The designers, whose collections I shall be seeing, will have visited the fabric shows in September/October 1987 and will have spent the time since creating their collections.

It comes as a surprise to many that, to a very large extent, it is the *fabric* manufacturers who dictate what we shall be wearing: if they produce fabrics that are more fluid, the designers cannot produce tailored clothes; if they decide that there have been enough blacks and browns, they will say we are ready for something else; if a lot of checks have been around, they might decide that we should go into spots or stripes. The fabric manufacturers, like any designer, have to sell their goods, so are constantly having to come up with something new. They have a great deal of power.

Once the designer has seen the fabrics, he or she will produce samples of designs utilizing those fabrics, and only after the collection has been shown and all the orders collated, will the total fabric order be confirmed. Some designers pre-buy fabrics – either for safety or for exclusivity – and it's always obvious to us that they have done so as the 'selling' of the fabric is so enthusiastic! After these fabric orders have been made firm in March, the fabrics are manufactured, the designs are made up, and we at Wardrobe could expect to see about half the clothes we have ordered in March arriving in our shops from around July, with the remainder in September. This is not very long for some very complicated processes (and there is many a slip twixt initial order and delivery).

Meanwhile, the designers, in about April (a few weeks after their current collection), will go again to the fabric shows, to see the fabrics to be used in their collections for spring and summer of 1989. These we will see in October of 1988, again at Milan, and we would expect delivery of completed clothes in about March. At Wardrobe we have two or three major designers and about five or six others. The latter we will see in March and October, but we will see the major designers' collec-

'I used to have far too many clothes, although I always complained that I had nothing to wear! A large amount of time and money was spent on clothes, which would then be taken home, hung up and rarely worn. I had no idea what clothes I owned, because too many of them in the wardrobe couldn't be seen.'

Stephanie Ellis,
Civil Servant

tions rather earlier in the buying year, in January and July, as we have to buy *more* (just as designers do from fabric manufacturers) if we want to maintain an exclusivity.

When I set off to buy for a season (which is at least eight months ahead), I have no definitive knowledge of what I am going to see. I have no idea whether the skirts will be long or short, or what colours will be in. However, because of my experience in the business, I will be aware of and can recognize trends. For instance, at the moment we've had two seasons of short skirts and I think it likely there will still be more short than long, because short skirts took longer to become popular this second time. There will be a few longer skirts for those who don't want to wear the short, and to further cater for this group I am expecting to see some new shapes of trousers. Designers have to give women alternatives, otherwise they won't buy – and the fashion business can't afford for that to happen.

As for colour, as there have been a lot of greys, blacks and browns for a long time I am expecting to see some bright colours for next winter. These will mainly be in blouses and sweaters, but there will also be a few bright suits amidst the neutrals (for those lucky enough not to have to wear a suit for more than one season). The fabrics will probably be fluid and hard-wearing – there's a resurgence of jersey at the moment, for instance – and I can expect to see softer knitted suits which look rather like dresses and are therefore more feminine. I also think I shall be seeing a lot of different accessories.

When we arrive in Milan, we go to a huge centre where there are perhaps 2,000 stands on which designers show their wares; the clothes themselves are on rails or on mannequins. These stalls show the *prêt à porter* or cheaper collections; the high fashion designers have their own showrooms. I always walk up and down the aisles for a day or two, to get a feel of what's happening. Some stalls I might go into to take a close look; some I wouldn't bother with as it is immediately obvious that it's not my style of merchandise. I would then go to the major designers' showrooms to see what they are offering. There are some designer showrooms I wouldn't be admitted to as I do not sell their clothes. For, in order to offer exclusivity, major designers only have one or two, perhaps three, stockists in one city – in that price range, the customer doesn't want to bump into another identical suit or dress!

Once I see something I like, I go in, tell them who I am, where I come from, and they will inform me about other stockists in London and whether they are prepared to supply me. Then I look around some more, try the clothes on, mention reservations if any, and start to buy – bearing in mind all the while the characteristics and sizes of my customers, what the garments look like, who they will sell to, what colours I sell well, how many of the garments I think I can sell, what fabrics I think the garments will look best in and will sell best, and whether the price is right.

This moment is critical to my business, and it can be very traumatic trying to keep so many considerations and criteria in the forefront of my mind. If I buy too many of one garment, I won't be able to sell them and capital is tied up; if I buy too *few* of a garment, I could lose out on a lot of profit by not having enough of a popular style. And if the colour or fabric is wrong, I could be in trouble as well. At the moment, for instance, green is a particularly fashionable colour, but I don't consider it right for my market as the British tend to associate green with school uniforms! You have to be very, very careful not to get carried away by salesmanship, media hype or sheer passion (if I'd given in this season, my shops would have been full of nothing but the most magnificent coats). Once you've placed the order and signed, you've made your commitment, and if the designers don't want to accept a cancellation, they are under no obligation to do so.

I'll give you a further idea of some of the problems. In our own collection, for example – the Wardrobe Italia label – we have probably six shapes of jacket and three shapes of skirt which we can put together depending on the proportions. We will probably have around twenty different fabrics, so we have to work out in our minds what fabric will look best in which style. There might be ten that would look good in one particular style, but we've got to decide which will look *best*. No-one can help us make these decisions – it's all a combination of experience, knowledge of our customers and what they're going to like, and our own gut reactions. It's all very mentally taxing, as is everything in this frenetic period of just under a week, so decisions depend on experience and a quickness and sureness of eye.

As we're ordering from *one* designer, we have to tally with what we've ordered from *other* suppliers. We keep a log, and at the end of every day we balance out our buying into how many coats, skirts, dresses, etc we've bought that day, and total them so that we can see the ratio of dresses to jackets, etc, and work out whether we have enough top halves for bottom halves. It's rather like fitting together a jigsaw puzzle! The colours have to be right too, both in terms of what the customers like, and what is fashionable – but they must be right for the shop as well. It's yet another consideration; if there are too many colours together haphazardly in the shop, the shop itself would look rather a mess. (Our shops are small, so we don't want to buy in bulk just in order to have more attractive swathes of colour.)

The clothes ordered in March will, as I said, start coming in July, with the bulk coming in September. In the shops, we therefore have rather a short time in which to sell that winter's collection – from September to November. Most shops are on

'Style is nothing, but nothing is without its style.'

Antoine Rivaral

sale in December. For the summer collections, we have from January to June in which to sell. This short time in the autumn can spell disaster. If a collection is delivered late a shop might be virtually empty of stock during an important selling period and could stand to lose enormous amounts of money. Delays are endemic in the fashion business, though: many are due to the fabrics (if they have flaws once made up, the garments will have to be sent back); if there's a lorry, train or port authority strike, we're stymied; if the trimmings people don't deliver the buttons on time, whole collections can be sitting there, unable to be delivered.

Once the clothes arrive in the shops, the problems might still not have ended. Jackets could arrive, but not the skirts or trousers to go with them – and that means the jackets are unsaleable until the skirts arrive. Once we had a delivery of knitted silk suits with top and bottom halves from different dye lots, so they all had to go back, leaving us lacking 36 suits which we'd raved about to our customers.

Another problem – perhaps the largest that any fashion retailer suffers – is that the merchandise can differ from the original sample. We try on the samples when we talk to designers for a very good basic reason – to see that the garment *works*. If we think there is a flaw, we place our order on condition that they consider and rectify it. For exactly the same reason, when the clothes come into the shop, we try them on *again*. This is how we discovered once that a collar rise on a jacket was an inch higher than it had been on the sample. If we hadn't tried the jacket on, we would have lost a lot of sales, simply because the collar would have been *uncomfortable*. However expensive a garment, it's made on a machine, supervised by someone who might be tired. Those slightly misshapen clothes you are always seeing in shop sales are manufacturers' errors which the buyer didn't pick up.

Once the clothes come into the shop, our customers are informed by letter or telephone and we place advertisements in the national press. If our buying has been intelligent, the clothes will walk off the racks and we can congratulate ourselves on having bought a successful collection. If our buying included some risk factors – something really unusual, or really expensive – they might take longer to go, but I still think that's worth it, otherwise I would end up with a shop full of very, very safe merchandise. And I don't think that's what my customers necessarily want: even though the suit they buy is for work, they like to be up to the minute; they don't want to be bored. Even if you're left with some stock at the end of a season, it needn't necessarily be a disaster, as you might be able to re-make. We cut some cotton trousers from last summer to mid calf length – we're ahead of fashion on this – and they're walking out of the shop!

'Fashion should indicate a way of thinking, not just a way of dressing.'

Giorgio Armani,
Fashion Designer

CHAPTER TWELVE

CLOTHES CARE

If you care about your appearance and want to look well-groomed, then regular wardrobe maintenance is a must. Your clothes and accessories will last longer, and you will save time because everything in your wardrobe will be immediately wearable. To keep clothes in top-notch condition, have a weekly wardrobe check, on a Sunday night perhaps. Cast your eye over your clothes, shoes and bags, and decide what needs cleaning, mending or pressing. This need only take half an hour, and you can go to work on Monday morning knowing that you are 'well maintained' for the week ahead!

SORTING

Hang clothes up as soon as you take them off, and put them somewhere to air before returning them to the wardrobe. Creases will fall out of most fabrics if the garment still retains heat from your body. Don't leave things in the pockets, because this pulls the garment out of shape. Give your clothes a good brush to remove bits of dust and fluff that might have accumulated during the day. An outfit in a plain fabric will always need brushing, because it will show specks more clearly than patterned fabric. Velcro-type material pads seem to be more efficient than traditional bristle brushes.

Hang up all your clothes apart from sweaters, T-shirts and lingerie. Store in the wardrobe with plenty of space between garments so that they do not crumple. Wire coathangers can damage shoulderlines and are too insubstantial for most outfits, so use chunky wooden or plastic ones. Wooden hangers with a serrated lower bar covered in rubber are most useful for hanging trousers, because they will not slip off. Even belts are best stored hanging from the buckles – they are less likely to 'crack' than if they are stored rolled up. Leather skirts are an exception; they have a tendency to 'seat' and are often best stored rolled up to help them regain their shape.

Bear in mind when you are designing or choosing storage space for your bedroom, that shelves in a cupboard are a lot more useful than drawers. Sweaters can get squashed and the fibres damaged when they are stored in drawers. Shelves are useful, too, because you can see at a glance exactly what you have, rather than having to root about. Drawers and shelves should be lined so that splinters of wood do not damage clothes. Lavender sachets can keep lingerie sweet-smelling.

Store your bags and shoes to help them keep their shapes. You should put shoe trees in your shoes whilst they are still warm. When you buy handbags they are often stuffed with paper and, if you want to store them for some time you could refill them with paper to help them keep their shape.

Life can be made much more efficient if you store your clothes according to the seasons. In the moderate climate of Britain, for instance, there are roughly two 'dressing' seasons, winter and summer, so you should move summer clothes to the most accessible spaces in the wardrobe or drawers in summer; the same with the winter selection in winter. Store the clothes that are out of season at the back of your wardrobe, or in a little-used drawer or zipped plastic bag if space is tight. This moving of your clothes twice a year is usually a good opportunity for your wardrobe evaluation (see page 47)!

'Always be well-dressed, even when begging.'

Hindu Proverb

CLEANING

Bad dry-cleaning can curtail the life of a garment, whilst first-rate cleaning will prolong it. I get most of my clothes dry-cleaned because, like many women, I don't dislike ironing but can never find the time to do it. I also think the professionals do it better! I always attach notes to the clothes describing any stains and exactly what they are. It is also worth pointing out shoulder pads, otherwise you risk the garment being returned with two scrunched-up, cotton-wool like balls! If you are uncertain whether the buttons on a garment will survive dry-cleaning then mention that too, and a good dry-cleaner will remove them if necessary. Similarly with belts.

The extent to which you dry-clean your clothes rather than wash them depends on your personal preference and your budget. Many women prefer to wash clothes because they feel that they are cleaner and smell fresher. Certainly, the worst sort of cleaners do not change the chemical solution very often, so there is always the possibility that your clothes have been cleaned in rather dirty liquid which gives them a gritty texture. When washing clothes, though, they still get a 'beating', so always make sure that your washing powder dissolves well, and that you rinse thoroughly. Follow the advice on the garment, on your powder packet and on the washing machine instructions. If hand washing more delicate fabrics, use soap flakes or liquid soaps.

Use specialist cleaners for leather and suede garments. Some cleaning companies will pick up clothes and then deliver them back. They are slightly more expensive than a high-street dry-cleaner, but not as much as you might expect for such high standards and convenience factors – a boon for the busy working woman. Beware of cleaning services in hotels; even in America I have not found them to be of a very high standard.

Use the polythene bags your newly cleaned clothes come in to protect clothes that you do not wear often – like evening wear. If travelling, keep your clothes in the bags to help them stay crease-free.

If something gets stained, then resist the temptation to douse the stain with water. It is often more difficult to get the stain out afterwards and often you lose the colour from the fabric, even some cottons can fade if splashed with water. Some of the stain-removing chemicals on the market now are quite effective. If you are uncertain, and the garment is a cherished one, then opt for the best dry-cleaning that you can afford.

Keep bags and shoes regularly polished, and use the most suitable products to clean them with. If you can, always clean shoes *before* you put them away rather than trying to find the necessary five minutes in the morning: the polish can be feeding the leather overnight. Suede shoes can lose colour very quickly at the toe-caps. If they are in black or dark brown, buy some suede dye and regularly dye that part of the shoe. The dye will also cover the sole toe-cap which easily scuffs. With lighter coloured suede, there can be difficulty in matching the tone of dye to that of the shoes. So be careful.

'Fashion. A despot whom the wise ridicule and obey.'
Ambrose Bierce,
The Devil's Dictionary

PRESSING

One of my most useful acquisitions in recent years has been a pressing machine; it's semi-professional – basically a steam box with an iron on it – and made in Italy. You can use it to press vertically or horizontally, and I use it for all my tailored clothes and my husband's suits.

Pressing sleeves can be quite tricky. Roll up a medium-sized towel and stuff it into the sleeve; you can then press the sleeve evenly all over, so that it is free of unsightly creases. I also press leather skirts to help them keep their shape; *very, very* carefully, though, with a towel covering the leather.

Spray starches are useful for crisping up cotton collars and cuffs and linen clothes. If your clothes could do with pressing, but you are in a hurry or have no iron, then hang them in your bathroom at home or in your hotel room. The steam will help the creases to drop out. (Steam is also good for smoothing out velvet.) Never wear your clothes immediately after pressing them. If the fabric is still warm, it will crease very quickly indeed, undoing all your good work.

Bows and trimmings on lingerie often wrinkle during washing. After you've squeezed the moisture out of your favourite bra and pants, smooth out the bows and trimmings with your fingers so that they are lying flat. They should dry as new and need no pressing.

If you really hate ironing or pressing, you can always find some enterprising person who can do it *for* you, a service quite commonly available now.

REPAIRS

Try and effect repairs as soon as they need doing. If you put them to one side, the next time you go to wear the garment you'll waste precious minutes making it presentable. Even small details like a label coming undone should be attended to, otherwise it could stick up above your collar. If a button drops off, sew it on as soon as possible, or you'll lose it.

Keep a mini repair kit in the office, with some needles, thread in neutral colours (depending on the predominant shades in your wardrobe), safety pins and buttons. For safety, carry the same in your toilet bag when travelling.

USEFUL ADDRESSES

Fill in the blank spaces as a handy reference guide.

Hairdresser _____

Colourist's name _____

Manicurist _____

Chiropodist _____

Beauty Salon _____

Make-up Consultant _____

Aromatherapist _____

Fitness Centre _____

Yoga Classes _____

Relaxation Classes _____

Massage _____

Nutritionist _____

Clothes Shops _____

Shoe Shops _____

Leather Goods _____

Dry cleaner _____

Invisible mender _____

Doctor _____

Optician _____

Dentist _____

Hygienist _____

USEFUL BOOKS

FLYING HIGH: THE WOMAN'S WAY TO THE TOP
Liane Jones, *Fontana*, (1987)

YOUR BRILLIANT CAREER
Audrey Slaughter, *Macdonald Optima* (1987)

MANWATCHING: A FIELD GUIDE TO HUMAN BEHAVIOUR
Desmond Morris, *Granada* (1978)

BUSINESS AMAZONS
Leah Hertz, *Deutsch* (1986)

THE DEVIL'S DICTIONARY
Ambrose Bierce, *Penguin* (1971)

THE PROFESSIONAL IMAGE
Susan Bixler, *Perigree Books, USA* (1984)

THE SIXTIES IN QUEEN
Ebury Press (1987)

DRESS AND UNDRESS. A HISTORY OF WOMEN'S UNDERWEAR
Elizabeth Ewing, *Batsford* (1978)

A FASHION FOR EXTRAVAGANCE
Sarah Bowman, *Bell and Hyman* (1985)

THE SECOND SIN
Thomas Szasz, *Routledge* (1973)

PATOU
Meredith Etherington Smith, *Hutchinson* (1983)

THE LANGUAGE OF CLOTHES
Alison Lurie, *Heinemann* (1982)

WOMEN: DRESS FOR SUCCESS
John T. Molloy, *Foulsham* (1980)

IN FASHION
Prudence Glynn and Madeleine Ginsburg, *Allen & Unwin* (1978)

PERSONAL STYLE
James Wagenvoord, *Holt, Rinehart and Winston, USA* (1985)

WARDROBE

For further information about the shops,
seminars and consultancy contact:

Wardrobe
3, Grosvenor Street,
London W1
telephone 01–629 7044
or
17, Chiltern Street
London W1
telephone 01–935 4086

S F E R A

The new WARDROBE perfume
'The sweet smell of success'

My 'Thank You' Page

My sincere thanks to everyone involved in this book for all their hard work and professionalism. I am delighted with the result.

There are a few special 'thank you's' I would like to say;

To my sons Richard and James who have always been a great source of love, pride and support to me.

To Mum and Dad for their love and understanding – I know that as a child I drove them mad with my very determined views on appearance!

To Philippa Davies (Pippa) for her enthusiasm and hard work and for the enjoyment I had working with her.

To Gill Cormode (from Piatkus), for her strong guidance, dedication and gentle manner. I learnt a lot.

To my friends and colleagues at Wardrobe, for their loyalty, support and understanding. A terrific team to work with.

INDEX

Note: page numbers in italic refer to illustrations